Jews Did Count

But For the Wrong Reasons

A Lament

By
Simon Cohen

MAPLE
PUBLISHERS

Jews Did Count But for the Wrong Reasons

Author: Simon Cohen

Copyright © Simon Cohen (2023)

The right of Simon Cohen to be identified as author of this work has been asserted by the author in accordance with section 77 and 78 of the Copyright, Designs and Patents Act 1988.

First Published in 2023

ISBN 978-1-915796-41-7 (Paperback)
      978-1-915796-42-4 (E-Book)

Book Cover Design and Layout by:
      White Magic Studios
      www.whitemagicstudios.co.uk

Published by:
      Maple Publishers
      Fairbourne Drive, Atterbury,
      Milton Keynes,
      MK10 9RG, UK
      www.maplepublishers.com

This book is dedicated to fellow sufferers of M.E and those struggling with mental health issues whilst living in a world that worships the ceaseless energy of ambition. It is also dedicated to those who, often silently, challenge the crushing narratives that brook no dissent in a society, as the Jewish writer Elias Canetti put it, that 'is choking on power.'

Contents

It is not the struggle of opinions that has made history so violent, but rather the struggle of belief in opinions, that is, the struggle of convictions. If only all those people who thought so highly of their conviction, who sacrificed all sorts of things to it and spared neither their honour, body nor life in its service, had devoted only half of their strength to investigating by what right they clung to this or that conviction, how they had arrived at it, then how peaceable the history of mankind would appear! How much more would be known!
(Nietzsche: Human, All Too Human)

Acknowledgements

Suffering from M.E can often mean that one lives a fairly isolated life, hemmed in by limits on energy; days often spent in a blear of fatigue; feeling elementally clapped out and scrap-heaped; the expression *burnt out* not a figure of speech but a real, physical phenomenon. Some days are better than others, where perception seems lighter and clearer and things can be done: ploughing on with writing, playing a Bach fugue with a cautious sense of emerging pleasure or just simply enjoying not feeling as gutted and wasted as a few hours ago. Struggling with O.C.D as part of the 'package' also creates a daily mental obstacle course with it's trip wires, mine fields and mental bombardments that are intent on negating functional living in the world as it is constituted. This is another depletion on energy, a vicious cycle where the mind is constantly trying to snooker itself or create an inescapable stalemate.

Writing a book, albeit a rather short one, under these conditions is quite a challenge and despite my general isolation, cut of from any stimulating academic and intellectual environments and even a basic social life that might offer more feedback, fraternity and contextual framework, I have been appreciative of having received words of encouragement from a few friends. In particular, my daily contact with Karen, a dear and close friend who has always stood by me despite the trials and frustrations of doing so. Due to distance and the prevalence of M.E in both our cases, contact is now limited to the telephone but is, still, a vital form of support. I would also like to thank Gerard, a recent acquaintance made in my newly adopted condominium, who has offered encouragement and conversation despite his occasional discomfort with and limited concurrence with some of the ideas and stances contained in this book. In many ways he manifests something whose decline I lament in the present offering.

I have been also encouraged by my mother and sister, not through discussions specifically related to the writing of this book but through their personal spirit which refused to accept the dominant antisemitism narrative. That my mother, aged 87 at the time, could still vote for social and economic change when the voices of her friends and acquaintances were, almost to a person, echoing the media narrative, was impressive. My son, David, has also offered encouragement along the way. He is in the process of completing his degree in the politics of the Middle East and is a politically aware young man in a world of rapid change and unsettling developments. The last few years have shown that it is with our young people that the hope of change resides. My generation acceded to the 'greed is good' mantra and drank the neoliberal '*Kool Aid*' (to use an Americanism) too readily.

Sometimes one comes across a book that encapsulates thoughts and ideas, hovering at the level of pure feeling, often for many years, that one was never able, through lack of the necessary skills and mental acuity, to bring into shape enough to express clearly in any external form. Such a book, for me, is Enzo Traverso's *The End of Jewish Modernity*. This short book is a small masterpiece that clarified, in its dense and rich prose, what had changed within the Jewish communities, how and why a certain cultural richness has been lost and why so much of the mainstream element of those communities has become absorbed, as I see it, into the *status quo*. Where were the questioners, the radicals, the anarchistic spirits, the mavericks, the marginalised thinkers, the dissenters, the non-comformists? What role did Zionism play in this transformation, with its hard-wired notion of Jewish identity, it's role as a Right Wing, populist State, recruited into the so-called 'clash of civilisations' paradigm? This gem of a book touched on all of this, itself almost an expression of the lost world it talks of but in valedictory form. The only other book that I have encountered that conveyed such a valediction, albeit through the form of the novel, was W.G. Sebald's *Austerlitz*, its main figure a Central European Jew who has to piece his own past together like a private detective, the rediscovery of *this* lost world resulting in a floundering sense of self precipitating the collapse of his psyche. As I see it, Traverso's book is to the loss of Jewish cultural richness and intellectual vitality as Sebald's is to this tragic loss of this Jewish modernism within the framework of the European tradition itself, expressed through the prism of a Jew retracing his connection to the heart of this Europe. Both these books, it seems to me, are laments of a sort. In my own inept and inadequate way, so is this one. Despite not having the skills, academic background and capacity to write the book I wanted to, the present one will have to do. What has passed, in recent years in the UK required me to at least raise my voice as best I could.

A mention should also go to a small group of those on Twitter who offered support and a valuable form of fellowship. As I discuss in more detail in the Postscript of this book, Twitter can be a polarising and antagonising environment but at its best can offer very meaningful interactions. As I don't know their real names (unless part of the 'handle') I would like to mention the following, in no particular order, who have been supportive and intelligently informative: 'Daddy_cOo1; @Grombags; @simonmaginn; @CasperBryson; @TweetForTheMany; @HavetStorm. Apologies to others not mentioned here who have played a helpful role. Of course, their being mentioned here implies no automatic concurrence with the content of this book.

All the viewpoints represented in this book are, of course, entirely my own, likewise any mistakes of a factual nature. Trying to write whilst suffering from M.E obliges one to be operating continuously on the edge of what one's energies will permit to the point of questioning whether the task at hand is even a realistic proposition. Hopefully, these difficulties have not entirely marred the text too much or rendered too vague and opaque that which I wanted to get across.

Introduction

It actually hurts physically thinking of the hope we all had back then and how things are now. Seeing this man get destroyed and who now leads the Labour Party has left me feeling there really is no way out of this. We're all going to suffer the rise of fascism again because even with all the historical warnings we failed the test[1]

The last twelve years have shocked me to the core. I was repeatedly shocked at what our society permitted during this period and I was shocked that we all weren't shocked more than we were. The shocks came thick and fast and I was shocked each time, not just by how little shocked we were but also by the level of callous revelling, from some quarters, in the cruelty meted out. Something had changed in our society and although I was more than aware of the effects of the crass economic ideology that dominated us like some great *'vampire squid,'* I had naively underestimated its deeper effects in penetrating the world of thinking and feeling of many of my fellow citizens. I began to feel the world around me had partly become a scenario from a Zombie film. I had always thought that the Zombie obsession of the *'Noughties'* was reflecting something about societal change and this fully revealed itself during the next decade. There was much use of the term 'zombie economics' to describe the dominant ideology that kept promising a 'trickle down' of wealth that never happened and furnished the opposite. But the word 'zombie,' to me, had a much wider meaning. I was permeated by a feeling of a growing sense of numbness and vacuity of the culture around me which became menacing and alienating to some extent.

The first shock that struck me, possessing a taser-like hit, was the response of the Tory Government to the financial crisis of 2008 which was

---

1   Comment by *Reluctant Socialist* below Double Down News video, on *Youtube* of Jeremy Corbyn speaking about being vindicated by the *Forde Report*.

brought about by an out of control financial system that had glutted itself on debt instruments, thinking it could spin these plates indefinitely after years of feeding off a housing bubble and supplying debt to consumers whose wages would have been other wise too low to maintain aggregate demand. This was a 'trick' learnt in the 80's as a method of keeping wages low, corporate profits high whilst allowing consumers, as carriers of debt, to keep the economy going. It was "bankers heaven," as economist Richard Wolff called it[2]: Banks were, in effect, renting out the currency to the low-waged public and increasingly making profits off soaring house prices. Yet when it collapsed, after initial Tory blandishments by the then newly elected Prime minister, David Cameron that "the broadest shoulders should bear a greater load,"[3] there soon followed a thorough grooming of the population, using propaganda techniques of a near Goebbels-like nature, to create a framing that it was the poor, ill and vulnerable who were to blame for pulling the economy down. Ministers tested the waters, very cautiously at first, by inserting deprecatory phrases about welfare claimants at suitable points in their interviews, the frequency increasing in proportion to their perception of the degree to which the populace was swallowing the narrative. Many of us will recall the phrases used:

"Those that get up in the morning."

"Those with their blinds drawn"

"Strivers and skivers."

This tepid introduction of that framing was due to a certain lack of surety about the potential efficacy of this line, so there was, initially, a short period of tentativeness concerning whether this bait would be taken. They didn't have to wait long for 'positive' signs. Soon the confidence increased as the Tories realised this narrative was popular with the public and the attacks on welfare claimants, as a result, became ever more brazen and bullish. So this was my first gut-wrenching shock: I never thought it was possible that so much of the populace would imbibe this as if it were some

---

2   See: Richard Wolff, Capitalism Hits the Fan, https://www.mediaed.org/transcripts/Capitalism-Hits-the-Fan-Transcript.pdf

3   https://www.theguardian.com/commentisfree/2010/oct/06/david-cameron-conference-speech-verdict it's rather 'touching' to read this now, before people really knew what was coming. The proto-fascism was soon to follow, at this point disguised by weasel words about 'fairness' and the bogus notion of 'the big society,' which latter soon meant charities, in particular food banks, replacing social services.

sort of elixir. And as I witnessed this happening together with the *Welfare Reform Act* of 2012 which consolidated this attack on welfare claimants, I reeled with the shock that the financial elite could have brought the economy to its knees whilst the public, in significant numbers, gladly acceded to a narrative that it was the ill and vulnerable that were pulling this economy down. Something bizarre had happened. What was it? I can vividly remember a *'below the line'* comment under a Guardian article at that time where a commenter, in a state of incredulity commensurate to my own, simply stated: *"What's happened to my country?"* It was good to know that others were also shocked and dismayed yet the Government narrative predominated and it soon became clear to me that its chief design feature was to create a wedge between the 'struggling in-work' and the unemployed and disabled, who were deemed to be 'scroungers and freeloaders.' It seemed that the Tories had discovered fertile ground for channelling justified anger and resentment in entirely the wrong direction. I never thought for a second that this would 'wash.' Indeed, I was expecting it to be so forcefully rejected and deemed utterly risible that the Government would be forced to backtrack fast. The exact opposite was the case, the Government had struck propaganda gold. It was a clear sign that we were entering a *'proto-fascist'* period, often ascribed to the post-Brexit period, but clearly manifest by 2013. This was the first whiff of fascism, that is, a propaganda program to scapegoat those who were the weakest and most powerless in society and deflect attention away from the financial class to whom many of these Government ministers were connected and whose interests they clearly wanted to preserve as they were aligned with their own.

A feature of my own sense of shock was the subsidiary shock that this was so easy to do and the bogus narrative sold like hot cakes. How could this happen? Why wasn't there a roaring *"no, we're not having that?"* As I looked into these questions I realised that I had to take into account how the society I grew up in had been transformed over the previous forty years. Something whose extent I had neglected to seriously consider. I knew I had to look into the economic history of the last forty years and weigh up the sustained effect of the dominant economic myths of our time and how they had changed patterns of thinking and expectations. This entailed a great deal of reading especially with regard to the nature of our monetary system and the many myths about Government spending capacity that abounded in the public consciousness. Something was needed to explain how a bunch of largely public schoolboys were able to pull off such a transparent stunt and groom much of the public to believe things that were manifestly false. As I reeled with the shock and deepened awareness of what was clearly an extremely right wing and vicious stance realising itself in front of me, I also tuned into the deeply disturbing reality that most of the media were propping up the myths, arguable lies and corrupt ideological discourse. A seminal moment for me was watching an interview on the BBC with the then Chancellor George Osborne which was of such mind bending vapidity, lacking any form of serious challenge to the amateurish justifications for austerity that I decided to ditch my T.V license on the spot, cancelling the license fee and giving my television to a charity. The removal of the television from my lounge symbolising my severance from the mainstream media for good. It was a health giving purge. This was in 2014 as the assault on welfare and the imposition of the bedroom tax was further denigrating and demeaning some of the most fragile and vulnerable in our society. This was another shock that left me reeling: our media was complicit in propping up the whole show in the most egregious way. The ridding myself of the television and license fee fulfilled my resolution that I was not going to give a *'bent farthing'* in assistance to the state broadcaster that had become the equivalent of *Pravda* or the *Tass Newsagency* on an especially bad day.

The Chancellor at that time, George Osborne, seemed to epitomise this whole seedy, insidious, oleaginous, slimy and sub-reptilian culture that was grooming the populous. This ex-Eton character who, when initially taking on the job, seemed rather shy and diffident, probably due to his lack of knowledge of economics and inherent lack of qualifications other than class connections, showed increased confidence as the *"those that get up in the morning"* propaganda program gathered pace and acceptance. It was sickening to see this pipsqueak of a public schoolboy with his sly, surreptitious, furtive grin that was more like a seedy leer, lording it over the public and casually doling out suffering like someone stuck in a cruel phase of childhood thrusting a stick into an ants' nest and feeling a god-like power as they watched the ants scurrying manically. He came across to me as a cheap public school bully who paid others to do the bullying while he looked through peepholes at the suffering of the victim, deriving some strange psycho-sexual satisfaction from it. It was hard to imagine how such a character could even stand in the political arena without being immediately seen as a scoundrel, fraud and driven out. Yet a significant section of the public seemed enamoured of these people. Found them charming and likeable. This section of the British public not only included those who were well *'financialised'* and benefiting from the asset bubbles of land and housing but also many who were struggling and in the lower percentiles of wealth who had probably imbibed the notion, so prevalent in meritocratic societies, that the difficulties they were facing were due to their own deficiencies, usually defined as a lack of 'ambition' and/or skill to become financialised and batten off the wealth siphoning system. 'Ambition' only had this one meaning and was drained of any other significance as a motivator of human activity. I became intensely aware that one significant effect of our monetary wealth-worshipping and celebrity obsessed culture had created a self-esteem crisis, an epidemic in fact that caused people to see those that were lording it over them as their superiors. We had returned to the forelock tug.

As I educated myself about economics, a subject that, in the past, had been an instant soporific and narcoleptic but now appeared a necessity, I gradually awoke to the way we were being paraded with panoplies of myths about government finances. The chief one that the Government propagated was the notion that the Government had *"maxed out its credit card."* This is known as a *"fallacy of composition,"* the mythical notion that a currency issuing Government could 'run out of money' and go bankrupt like a household or business when it is, in fact, the entity that issues the currency. More shocks and disbelief as this myth was propagated in a manner just short of frenzied. But to be fair, this was one area where it was less easy to accuse the public of being jejune and lazy, as these sorts of beliefs about Government finances had been repeated so much that they became embedded in the mind like a form of mental wallpaper. Thatcher's infamous statement that *the Government has no other money than that provided by taxpayers* was still taken as a truth despite being disprovable by asking the basic question: "if Government only has taxpayers' money, how did the Taxpayer's get it in the first place?" But no-one asked this basic question and took on trust the guff and flannelling that was being fed to them. The notion that the Government was financially constrained in this way was a major prop for justifying what must be called the abuse of the vulnerable and ill that carried on apace. Few questions were asked, we seemed to be living in times of extraordinary acquiescence on all fronts. It was deeply disturbing.

The attack on the ill and vulnerable became merciless, their function as a societal spittoon propped up by the mainstream media who flaunted rare and extreme cases of benefit fraud with the clear intention of conveying the impression that fraudsters were numerically significant. To some extent, the ground had been prepared by the previous Labour administration who brought in private firms to administer an increasing world of conditionality and constant assessment within the social security system, where fly-by-night companies extracted Government money in order to implement some short-term, hair brained scheme that not only helped no one but created a network of stressful obstacle courses for those already struggling with physical and mental health. The Tory government merely ran with the ball knowing that the scapegoating would be a useful conduit for displacement activity and decoying. By 2012-13, the years of the *Welfare Reform Bill* that ramped up the focussed attack on the most vulnerable groups in our society, a poll already showed that the general public perceived benefit fraud to be 27% of claimants despite the Department of Work and Pensions' own estimate being 0.7%! That the relationship between perception and underlying reality could be so skewed was a testimony to the effectiveness of political ideology and its propagation, assisted by the ever willing mainstream media. This link between the mainstream media and Government was transparent, blatant and "*in yer face*", yet the lies were believed by people in significant numbers. It was if, as Nietzsche put it, people were believing what was "seen to be believed" and whether there was any truth in it was irrelevant. It's quite likely that this was due to the need for a simple way of making sense of a situation that, to most people, would have appeared opaque and resistant to ease of explanation. Simplistic narratives clearly worked given a cultural environment where we have a largely dumbed-down press and television news reporting that 'lived down' to the pejorative description of its mechanical intermediary as an '*idiots lantern.*' The lack of real inquisitiveness should have been no surprise. Research also showed that politicians themselves had very little grasp of economics and the operations of the monetary system. Investigations by *Positive Money* showed that only about 10% of politicians had any inkling of how the banking system and the Central Bank operated[4]. And these largely came to false conclusions about it despite understanding some of the mechanisms.

---

4   https://positivemoney.org/2014/08/7-10-mps-dont-know-creates-money-uk/

Politicians seemed to have no interest in being educative and were mostly incapable of it anyway due to being uneducated themselves. An example of this was when the former Secretary of State for Work and Pensions, Iain Duncan Smith, maintained that the Corbyn led Labour Party's spending plans would result in the UK ending up technically bankrupt like Greece, not realising that the monetary system of the Eurozone was utterly unlike that of the UK treasury where bankruptcy was not an applicable concept. It was understandable that the general public should not necessarily understand this but for a politician this ignorance was like an engineer not knowing basic maths. The governing politicians were mere propagators of vacuous ideology; ideology that lined their wallets handsomely while spreading suffering whose resultant anger they calculatedly channelled in the wrong direction

Nothing new in that perhaps. But what appeared to be new was the almost universal collusion of the media as *"poverty porn"* and the *"skivers v. strivers"* narrative proliferated as television shows. This was something new, unsavoury and obsessive. Physical attacks on disabled people were being reported with greater frequency during this period. This, combined with an economic attack[5] on this very group, labelling them as some sort of burden on the economy fuelled resentment towards the vulnerable and openly channelled anger their way that should have been directed at the *real* causes. Research undertaken in 2015 by the *Disability Hate Crime Network* looking at motivating factors for these attacks indicated that the image of the 'benefit scrounger,' propagated implicitly and explicitly by Government played a significant role:

> *'Motivation varied widely, but 11 out of 60 comments on the incidents said attackers mentioned "benefits" or "scroungers". "I was verbally abused as a scrounger whilst shopping ... using a mobility scooter," said one respondent. "I was asked why I use a wheelchair sometimes, but sticks on other days. I tried to explain my condition varies from day to day. I was then told I was just fat and lazy and was doing it to get benefits," said another.'[6]*

5   https://www.theguardian.com/social-care-network/2017/nov/23/government-waging-war-against-disabled-people

6   https://www.theguardian.com/society/2015/jul/22/combat-disability-hate-crime-understand-people-commit

This was, perhaps, one of the most shocking manifestations of the effectiveness of the Government's propaganda. One felt a line had been crossed. Many, like myself, watched in disbelief but many, either applauded, remained indifferent or silent. It was as if the aforementioned exclamation of *"What's happened to my country?"* became a continuous, internal mantra that echoed constantly in my mind. Another below the line comment referred to the disabled and vulnerable as the new "Jews." A hyperbolic analogy perhaps, yet one that conveyed the nature of the scapegoating mechanism at work.

Despite the bleating of the austerity pushers that were telling us that cuts had to be made to reduce a deficit that didn't need to be reduced and was clearly too small anyway, the Government 'somehow' found money to pay for a huge increase of staff at the Department of Work and Pensions to monitor benefit fraud including staff walking streets with fake drink cans containing cameras.[7] Soon this redoubtable team was responding to vindictive and vexatious reports from those who had vendettas against others whose welfare claims were leveraged as a method of creating stress and upset whilst releasing a certain amount of personal frustration in the process. Societal spittoons work like that. This culture of 'grassing' seemed to become a sort of sport and form of *Schadenfreude*-ridden entertainment which at one time the cruelty of bear baiting or public floggings might have provided. The sense of proto-fascism was firming up with a certain sector of the public relishing their role as establishment stooges and snitches, feeding the bogus narrative of rampant fraud despite the fact that welfare was, in aggregate, vastly under-claimed.[8] The crazy irony was that Government spending was too low for the needs of the economy and small scale benefit fraud was, in fact, helping the creation of non- bank debt related money supply the real economy sorely needed. In this respect, the very small level of benefit fraud that existed was doing the real economy a favour – helping to keep local shops and services open in poorer areas of the country! This is not to say that fraud, in general, is to be encouraged, only that its effect in these limited cases, when coupled with an entirely unnecessary austerity, might well be considered an unintentionally positive contribution to the economy.

---

7   https://www.theguardian.com/society/2011/feb/01/benefits-fraud-investigators
8   https://theconversation.com/britains-unclaimed-benefits-four-million-families-miss-out-on-12-4-billion-84153

Job Centres soon became institutions aimed at handing out humiliating and punitive treatment. One user declared that they should be called 'sanction centres' as rumours abounded that centres were operating a culture of 'targets' in relation to shifting people off benefits by using sanctions even if it left them in total penury. Absurd reports appeared of people having their benefits stopped because they had to attend a funeral on the day of an interview. The instructions to sanction people for anything short of sneezing at the wrong time were clearly coming from the Office of the Secretary of State for Work and Pensions. The Government, of course, denied an explicit 'targets' culture but there was plenty of evidence that there was an *implicit* and draconian culture in Job Centres.[9]

This farcical extraction of the collective uric acid took a step further when Ministers suggested that the unemployed could be sanctioned for actually getting a job that was deemed to not be paid very well and indicative of a claimant lacking the go-getting drive and ambition that neo-liberal orthodoxy prescribed.[10] What were people to do? Train as investment bankers? Then there would be a glut of investment bankers whose wages would go down and concomitantly create a massive shortage of nurses, cleaners, bus drivers, care workers and a whole host of necessary key worker jobs. The logical fallacies and absurdities of all of this would have shamed a Mad Hatter's Tea Party! Yet, somehow, this UK version of the American Dream which the comedian George Carlin said was called a 'Dream' because 'you needed to be asleep to believe it,'[11] had some sort of currency with a populace that had, partially, absorbed Thatcher's notion that there was no society, only individuals scrambling to realise their self-interest. This, in turn, was a dehumanised version of Bentham's Utilitarianism where little collegiality played a role and a simplistic belief that the collective well being was the result of individuals chasing the chimera of their own happiness via financial wealth. The illogic of this is firmly demonstrated by the housing bubble where individuals chase personal financial wealth through ever increasing land and house

---

9   https://theconversation.com/fact-check-do-job-centres-have-a-target-for-benefit-sanctions-41212

10   https://touchstoneblog.org.uk/2015/03/benefit-sanctions-for-low-paid-workers/
     'In January this year [2015], in a move that received little media coverage at the time, this government introduced secondary legislation that would enable them to extend benefit sanctions to low paid workers who aren't doing 'enough' to earn more money.'

11   https://www.youtube.com/watch?v=kJ4SSvVbhLw

prices causing a transference of wealth to property owners and excluding more and more of those who cannot get on a 'housing ladder' whose rungs become ever more widely spaced until they are not there at all, wrecking communities and heaping debt burdens on succeeding generations. Yet housing wealth has been touted as the neo-liberal Nirvana for the last four decades at least, since the banking system discovered that it could make money, hand over fist out of this asset bubble.[12]

At every stage of the way I thought that there would be resistance. There was some, of course, yet the shock coursed through me as, increasingly, I had to accept that years of fragmentation and the sundered remnants of collegiality had given way to a strange, sealed off and calloused culture that had accepted the primacy of financial institutions whose major beneficiaries ran the show, determining our fate and well being. There were still significant elements of a co-operative nature but it was clear there was a divide in the populace between those that felt solidarity with the vulnerable and those drawn into seeing themselves in terms of the *individual maximiser of self interest* and *'winners'* who felt the system plucked out the 'fittest' in terms of their ability to make the system work for their benefit. The oft used Darwinian analogy was entirely inappropriate, for Darwin was using nature as his referent, not an economic system that was contingent. Within this framework of seeing the world, the ill, vulnerable and those that simply couldn't cope were seen as 'losers,' surplus population.

Another shock wave emanating from the neo-liberal, populist epicentre was the introduction of the so-called *Bedroom Tax* which was an attack on some 700,000 vulnerable, social housing tenants who had the temerity to have one or more spare bedrooms. This built, yet again, on the *'skivers/strivers'* meme that successfully, as it turned out once more to be, divided the in-work struggling with millstone mortgages against those who were perceived to have 'dodged' the housing bubble by obtaining increasingly scarce social housing. It was as if those in social housing were implicitly questioning the sense and reason of a life toiling with the cumbersome debt of a steaming great mortgage and they needed to be

---

12   The housing bubble we have now really began in the 70's with the relaxation of lending ceilings on banks. This sparked a housing bubble, the first of a long cycle that then accelerated after the deregulation of 80's. See: Phillip Whitehead, *The Writing on the Wall, Britain in the Seventies*, p. 94.

punished for the resultant uneasiness it created. The Sisyphean mortgage, that was such a boon for the banking system and the buy-to-let market could not be called into question and those carrying the millstone must be patted on the head and told they were '*doing the right thing.*' The Tories, at this point, expressed a transparently clear animus against social housing putting rent caps on Housing Associations that were designed to cripple them financially and force them to sell off properties, especially in areas where property prices were high.[13] The politicians on the Right (and generally on the so-called Left for that matter) never explained the roots of the housing crisis in terms of the history of the housing bubble which involved excessive bank lending for mortgages and buy-to-lets and land banking by developers that maximised land value and hence the resulting house prices. The housing bubble was taken as a state of nature and politicians like David Cameron gave his condescending approbation to those battling grotesque mortgages as doughty citizens that were '*doing the right thing.*' Yet again, an ex-Etonian who was plugged into wealth extraction and offshored wealth was allowed to speak condescendingly to the public with little anger or pushback. It was incredible to behold. Never, in my worst nightmares had I imagined such cowering quiescence. It seemed very clear that something had destroyed the self-esteem of much of the public over the previous forty years. One was a 'good boy' if you tugged your forelock in the presence of the financial moguls. Did getting patted on the head by these mega-wealthy, rich as Croesus wallet-liners confer some sort of selective serotonin reuptake inhibitor effect on those 'blessed' by their condescension? Did those struggling with low paid jobs and mill-stone mortgages feel a self-righteous rill as the quasi-Papal benediction from the world of financialised interests told them to gladly bear their cross, implying it was being a 'good citizen' whilst nodding in the direction of a soon to emerge populism that would also deem it 'patriotic' to be wrung through the financial system?

The Bedroom Tax, despite it being an assault on the most vulnerable in our society was popular as another channeller of resentment and *schadenfreude.* Both emotions that were the bedrock of neo-liberalism and the fueller of the divisions that sustained it. As someone who rented a housing association house that was deemed to have a 'spare room' I felt

---

13   https://www.newstatesman.com/politics/2015/07/governments-plans-are-nothing-short-attack-social-housing

the impact of this policy on both the financial and psychological level as the *vox pop* relegated me to the status of a failure, a scrounger, a person not '*doing the right thing.*' By not being plugged into the asset bubble and contributing to the siphoning by the banking system I was a non-person, an inferior, an economic *Dalit* who was not 'playing the game', the 'game' that the neo-liberals wanted to be the only game in town. It was as if you were not offering yourself to the financial body snatchers as a sacrificial victim, so you became a pariah. A psychopathology of this period is urgently needed.

Yet further shock waves radiated from the staggering inadequacy of the Opposition Party that was almost supine in its unresponsiveness: The Labour Party, seeing that the Bedroom Tax was popular and attacks on the vulnerable seemed to sell well, hummed and hawed for months before deciding to propose a policy to abolish it. It was introduced in the 2012 Welfare Reform Act and Labour only committed to its abolition in September 2013.[14] Meanwhile the shadow Work and Pensions Secretary, Rachel Reeves, was appropriating the punitive language of the Tories towards welfare claimants in order to surf the perceived electoral benefits of the scapegoating.[15] Perhaps it shouldn't have been a shock. Since Blair and Brown, the Labour Party had become, essentially, a party that propped up neoliberalism with its suppressed wages, housing bubbles and privatisations. The Party had already become known as '*Tory Lite*' and '*Labour in name only*' in Left leaning circles and there was an increased feeling of being in a one party state. As we have already noted, Blair and Brown's incumbency was distinguished by the outsourcing of welfare assessments to private companies who increasingly maintained questionable conditionality regimes that were implicitly dehumanising and designed to hammer people into the low wage and unaffordable housing culture of the wealth extractors.

As I read about the suffering caused by the Bedroom Tax, whilst being impacted by it myself, knowing it was transparently being used as a tool to channel discontent in entirely the wrong direction, I decided to try to find a *pro bono* solicitor to challenge the policy in court. I had heard of others

---

14 https://www.theguardian.com/politics/2013/oct/12/labour-benefits-tories-labour-rachel-reeves-welfare

15 https://www.theguardian.com/politics/2013/oct/12/labour-benefits-tories-labour-rachel-reeves-welfare

doing this and with some trepidation I made inquiries. To my surprise, I quickly got an offer to take on the case from *Liberty* solicitors who work to defend human rights and challenge the powerful to protect civil society.[16] This was the start of a long and complex process that eventually took us to the Administrative Court of the Royal Courts of Justice at the end of 2014, a journey lasting about a year and a half which inducted me into the world of legal systems as well as to the byzantine complexities of the work of barristers who generously gave their time to the cause. It was a real education. One of the most disturbing aspects of the legal challenges made to the Bedroom Tax was the way the Government appealed legal victories by those in extreme situations: people who were either disabled themselves and had equipment in a spare room and/or looking after disabled children that required a spare room for a carer. This prolonged psychological suffering and uncertainty in a life situation that was itself fraught and profoundly demanding both financially, physically and emotionally was a grotesque and capricious cruelty that further revealed how the 'red line' that demarcated what was acceptable in a decent society that respected human dignity had been crossed with substantial public approval. It constantly raised that same question: *"what has happened to my country?"* The Government spent hundreds of thousands appealing cases, lending credence to the belief that this was another strand of the "skivers/strivers" narrative that had nothing to do with 'saving money' but was part of an ideological drive as we have already noted. By June 2016, a study published in the *Journal of Public Health* made it clear that the policy worsened outcomes all round:

> *"The bedroom tax has increased poverty and had broad-ranging adverse effects on health, wellbeing and social relationships within this community. These findings strengthen the arguments for revoking this tax."*[17]

So the human cost, financially manifesting as costs in terms of health services resources was massively counter productive, yet the Government kept appealing legal decisions that challenged it with an almost mechanically vicious predictability. Clearly, they felt this disastrous

---

16 https://www.insidehousing.co.uk/news/news/bedroom-tax-faces-second-legal-challenge-35074

17 https://academic.oup.com/jpubhealth/article/38/2/197/1752995

policy, that did not do what it said on the packet and created social costs that were highly destructive was so important to them as a lynch pin of their project to create scapegoats that they were willing to create further egregious and gratuitous suffering to prop it up. By the end of 2015, the Government had paid out almost £500,000 appealing judgements that had gone against it. [18]

By now, my expectation that the shout of "NO!" from the British public would happen in some decisive way, was weakening considerably. I heard of individual acts of rebellion: the man who drove his car through the window of a job centre, thankfully only causing material damage[19]; the desperate man who self-harmed in a Job Centre, cutting at his own throat[20] and the man who incinerated his own flat after being pushed beyond despair by the Bedroom Tax.[21] There were, of course, more organised anti- Bedroom Tax protests but often, turn out was not overwhelming and I noticed mockery on social media and below-the-line comments under news reports of these events that reminded me that many considered people being affected significantly by austerity and Bedroom Tax as 'losers.' The callousing of society had become palpable and the political opposition was being forced to dance to, or dance around the dominant narrative. At the time of the introduction of the Bedroom Tax, a poll showed that 49% of voters supported it and 38% opposed[22]. Around the time that the Labour Party decided it would abolish the Tax, this had changed to 43% support and 45% opposed[23]. Other than showing that the Labour Party might well have been responding to slight changes in the *vox populi*, the poll was still dismaying given, by this time, there

---

18   https://www.belfasttelegraph.co.uk/news/uk/government-racks-up-near-500000-bill-fighting-bedroom-tax-cases-35241684.html

19   https://www.bbc.co.uk/news/uk-england-norfolk-22082552

20   https://www.dailymail.co.uk/news/article-2379984/Bedroom-tax-Man-slits-throat-benefits-advice-office-protest.html

21   https://www.mirror.co.uk/news/uk-news/bedroom-tax-victim-thulani-dlodlo-3249687

22   https://assets.publishing.service.gov.uk/government/uploads/system/uploads/attachment_data/file/255654/public-perceptions-of-rsrs.pdf 'There   is   higher support in principle for a reduction in the amount of Housing Benefit paid to those of working age in social housing if they have more bedrooms than the Government thinks they need. Almost half (49%) support a reduction, in principle, on these terms. However, opposition also increases to one-third (33%) of the British public.'

23   https://yougov.co.uk/topics/politics/articles-reports/2013/11/13/voters-now-divided-bedroom-tax

was significant awareness of the near calamitous suffering the policy was causing. It seemed to indicate that my sense of this callousing of society was more than a projection of my personal experiences and indicative of some sort of hard-wired division within the populous.

A significant surprise, for me, was still to arrive on the back of the sudden and unexpected blooming of hope with the election of Jeremy Corbyn as Labour Party Leader which brought with it the only political challenge to the neo-liberal hegemony since its onset nearly 40 years before. At first, his election was laughed at and seen as a joke, the Tories, initially considering his election as leader as an asset to them due to their belief that he would be unelectable nationally and only empower them the more. [24] Despite this superficial mockery due to an inability to conceive of any challenge to neoliberalism and the world of global finance, his election sent shock waves through the corridors of the establishment and the mainstream media set to work with a vengeance with daily vilifications and smears published in newspapers and the press crowded around Corbyn's modest house in Islington[25]. Worst of all insults to the establishment was Corbyn telling the press huddled around his gate that he never read them and that he would not seek their favours.[26] Perhaps this was one of the greatest taboos to break: refusing to do obeisance before the press, especially one that was predominantly Right Wing. Tony Blair, immediately after the 1997 election, had expressed a shameless, filial deference to the press, virtually bowing before Rupert Murdoch, their close connection expressing itself further as Murdoch made Blair godfather to one of his daughters. By 2018, Journalists Without Borders, who had been producing a yearly Press Freedom Index ranked the UK 40th out of 180 countries in their index, the very year that the smears, disinformation and daily vilifications of Corbyn had reached their fanatical, fervid and feverish peak. Almost the entirety of the British Press, including those

---

24 https://news.sky.com/story/no-laughing-matter-tories-change-tune-on-corbyn-10346450

25 Perhaps one of the more absurd and infinitely risible vilifications of Corbyn was the imputation that he was some sort of 'property baron' by dint of a fairly basic house in Islington bubbling furiously in value over forty years due to a bank lending induced asset bubble. https://www.dailymail.co.uk/news/article-3928436/Was-nuisance-neighbours-Terraced-house-door-Jeremy-Corbyn-s-Islington-home-sale-925-000-real-Champagne-socialist-afford-it.html

26 https://www.businessinsider.com/jeremy-corbyn-right-to-hate-the-media-video-him-being-assaulted-by-reporters-2015-9?r=US&IR=T

elements that were considered progressive had rounded up on the Leader of the Opposition making him the focus of their opprobrium, despite Corbyn's early insistence, after his election, that "It's not about me" as he attempted, with increased difficulty as the smears mounted, to keep the focus on the shift in economic ideology that he represented.

This ought to have been deeply shocking but was largely absorbed into the culture, becoming normative. And yet again, I was shocked that we were not collectively shocked that this could happen. Had neoliberalism and the fragmenting effect of its financialisation of everything pushed us all into an individualised survival mode so that the monolithic nature of the press and its ability to crush dissent was something hovering unquestioned above us as we scurried around trying to keep afloat? Had the financialised tail been wagging the dog for too long? These were questions I asked myself as I witnessed the most transparent and bogus of lies and forms of disinformation being seemingly soaked up like a sponge by significant sectors of the population. It's quite difficult to write these words which can easily sound condescending as I imply that whole swathes of the populous were merely vehicles for an establishment propaganda machine but it is quite difficult to put it any other way. I am, of course, fully aware that many people taken in by this surge of disinformation had their own reasons for believing it and were very decent people at the same time. Perhaps, in considering this historic period I have fallen into the trap the philosopher Hegel mentions when critiques of historical periods are too negative:

> 'For in passing negative judgements, one looks down on the matter in hand with a superior and supercilious air, without having gone into it thoroughly enough to understand its true nature...People often think they have done their job when they have found something which can be justly criticised; they are right, of course, in one respect; but they are also wrong in so far as they fail to recognise the positive factor.'[27]

Nevertheless, despite Hegel's belief in the progress of the Spirit through history, it was hard to discern anything in this situation being of spiritual value in itself unless the descent into a world of disinformation,

---

[27] Hegel, *Lectures on the Philosophy of World History*, Cambridge University Press, p. 66.

misinformation and the manipulation of knee jerk responses could be thought of as presaging some future transformation of a positive nature. If the latter is true then, to paraphrase Woody Allen, you 'wouldn't want to be there at the time' when the 'morbid symptoms' were manifesting themselves.

For me, the biggest shock was still to arrive and it came all singing and dancing and with bells on. The shock that is the subject of this book whose arrival has only been delayed by a generalised setting of the scene in order to frame its entrance which was like an intricately choreographed *Busby Berkely* dance routine. It came flying out of what seemed to be nowhere, becoming, eventually, the go to smear of smears whose currency seemed to increase in value over time to a press obsessed with making something stick that could ruin any hope of creating change in a country mired in austerity, low wages, scapegoating of the vulnerable and collapsing public services. I am, of course, referring to the apparent sudden emergence of antisemitism charges directed against Corbyn, the Labour Party and its membership in general. I say 'apparent' because, as we shall explore, in reality it had been waiting in the wings poised and charged to pounce on its hapless victims for some years. Given my Jewish background, it leapt out with greater personal relevance than all the other smears and vilifications. I'm already using the word 'smear' which in the eyes of many could daub me with the charge of 'antisemitism,' as even challenging the official narrative summons the very charge itself. The inherent '*truth*' of the charge being not susceptible to challenge is largely connected, as we shall also see later, to a basic misinterpretation of the *MacPherson Principle*. I'm using this word '*smear*', though, because I deem it an undeniable fact despite the charge of antisemitism against Corbyn and Labour having been slotted into history as an unassailable and rock hard verity.

Never before had I come across such a media interest in antisemitism. Prior to 2015 there was barely any mention of antisemitism in the media yet now the floodgates opened. Sure, the accusations emerged from time to time as in 2005 when the Labour Party was accused of it for depicting Oliver Letwin and Michael Howard as 'flying pigs,' a fairly banal and obvious use of a metaphor that turned out to be seen as highly non-kosher and their Jewishness incidental.[28] Yet even Claire Short's video meeting with Khalid Meshal, at that time Chairman of the Hamas Political Bureau

---

28   https://www.theguardian.com/politics/2005/feb/18/election2005.uk

and her meeting with him in Damascus with other M.P's and MEP's in 2009 did not cause such a whirlwind of media activity. Given that the flood of antisemitism allegations from 2015 were often raised by non-Jewish figures in the media, usually from right wing journalists, it was reasonable to be a little concerned about the sudden flurry of solicitousness over the sensibilities of what was perceived as the 'Jewish community'. Yet media figures and politicians scrambled to express their newly acquired concern for this historically calamitous form of violent prejudice and it was all focussed on the Labour Party despite a 2016 Select Committee inquiry stating clearly that there was no evidence that Labour "was overrun with antisemitism" or that it's prevalence was greater than in any other Party. Nevertheless, as Corbyn pointed out in response to the Select Committee's report:

> "Although the Committee heard evidence that 75 per cent of antisemitic incidents come from far right sources, and the report states there is no reliable evidence to suggest antisemitism is greater in Labour than other parties, much of the report focuses on the Labour party.[29]

Despite, as we shall see, a history of egregious antisemitism in the Tory Party which was to reveal itself further in the ensuing years up to the 2019 election, there was almost no concern expressed about the manifestations of antisemitism in that Party despite it occurring at high levels, including ministers and eventually a Prime Minister. Already, the largely media induced image that the Labour Party was "institutionally antisemitic" was gaining traction, despite absolutely no evidence that this was the case. In fact the expression "institutionally antisemitic" was being bandied around in a deliberately loose fashion despite the absence of any proof or inquiry to establish that case. In the end the serious allegation of "institutional antisemitism" was, rather, made for political purposes on the back of the accumulated weight of media reporting and hype designed to create the aura that could justify such a charge. What made the situation even more incoherent was that there was NO shared definition of antisemitsm that could create any boundaries around the valid use of the accusation other than references to the *Macpherson Prinicple* regarding racism and even

---

29   https://labourlist.org/2016/10/anti-semitism-report-violates-natural-justice-corbyns-response-to-mps-report/

this required the corroboration of independent evidence beyond the alleged victim's allegations. As we have already noted and will examine further, this *Principle* was thoroughly abused.

Over the next three years, this boundaryless notion of antisemitism grew to massive proportions, it's chaotic and irrational roots never looked at as it leveraged itself to such an extent that it achieved the status of an irrefutable truth. Although the *Macpherson Principle* enshrined the idea that it was the prerogative of the victim of perceived racism to initially define it's occurrence, the definition did not cover the politicised use of these accusations. Already, by 2016, the Labour Party was singled out as the focus for allegations of antisemitism despite, as we have observed, there being zero evidence there was any preponderance of it within the Party.

I was reeling with shock again and my naivety and lack of consciousness of the roots of these issues further exposed. Never had I thought it was possible to use antisemitism in such a blatantly politicised way. It felt like the historical tragedy of antisemitism was being cynically manipulated by the mainstream media in a manner that reminded me of the grooming of the public to swallow the myth that vulnerable welfare claimants were fraudsters who were bringing down the economy. I felt as if I had entered a world turned upside down; a collective plunging down the Alice in Wonderland Rabbit Hole:

"Down, down, down. Would the fall never come to an end!"

It was, perhaps, the last of a series of profound shocks that still reverberate within me and now motivate me to write this short book. The title of this book could be seen to be a reversal of meaning of the one used by David Baddiel for his book '*Jews Don't Count*' which is in my view, another inverted reality take on the antisemitism saga we'll be examining in these pages. It became very clear to me over that period of time that Jews, or some media created notion of Jews as a homogenised group, DID count but in a way that was not at all helpful to Jewish people nor for the preservation of a meaningful understanding of what antisemitism actually was. Many latched onto the realisation that antisemitism was being "weaponised," with those that did, themselves being accused of antisemitism. Jews like myself were being referred to as "self-hating" and "Kapos" whilst Tory antisemitism was ignored even when having been perpetrated by a Prime Minister. The Mad Hatter's Tea Party had arrived in all its gaudy craziness.

The ensuing chapters will explore my own responses to this incredible saga and the shock that led me to realise, not only how far to the Right the mainstream 'Jewish community'[30] had travelled but also how a minority of Jews bravely stood up to this mainstream to assert what I saw as the great Jewish Tradition of a Left that raised a challenge to the establishment and its 'manufacturing of consent.' I developed, perhaps, a somewhat romanticised image of those brave Jews, on the same path as the socialists and anarchists of yesteryear, who had inhabited a Yiddish speaking milieu (perhaps Yiddish was the ultimate anarchists' language!) of intellectuals and a literate working class who would dream of a better world built on freedom and social justice. That I realised I was largely alienated from the official institutions of what I vaguely saw, despite my universalism, as MY community had become clear when a poll showed that, in 2015, around 69 percent of the Jewish community had voted Tory[31] despite the manifest cruelties of its policies. This world was a far cry from the working class community of my parents in Manchester where, according to my father, people would meet in each other's houses to play music discuss politics, philosophy and the latest scientific developments; where ideas about progress and social equity were discussed. They met in houses situated within the rows of sere terraces a few miles from the city centre. My father, who would shout at the television every time a Tory appeared on it, hurling imprecations at the bulging box of analogue pyrotechnics in the corner of the living room, seemed to be where I thought the majority of the Jewish community was politically positioned. I realised that I had been asleep and not taken full cognisance of the extent of the changes that had taken place in the intervening 40 years. Just as the 2007-8 banking

---

30 In general, the expression *'Jewish community'* refers to those represented, or feel represented by the official Jewish institutions such as the Board of Deputies and the Office of the Chief Rabbi as well as the Jewish Labour Movement, the Labour Friends of Israel and the Campaign Against Antisemitism who all acted as the guardians of what was deemed antisemitism. In reality, we can only speak of *Jewish communities*, the term used by the historian of modern British Jewry, Geoffrey Alderman. See: G. Alderman, *Modern British Jewry.*

31 https://www.thejc.com/news/uk-news/huge-majority-of-british-jews-will-vote-tory-jc-poll-reveals-1.66001 This despite the possibility of a Jewish Prime Minister. The rejection of a potential Jewish P.M, was largely connected to the vote, in 2014, to symbolically recognise Palestinian statehood, a non-binding motion.

collapse had woken me up to the realities of the financialised world and its wealth siphoning mechanisms so, on a more localised and individual level, the politicised and geo-politicised use of antisemitsm woke me up to the changes in what I had considered my own community albeit one in which I was little engaged at the time and had not been for many years. Perhaps a premonition of this came when I was still at school in the late 70's when an Israeli teacher, in a moment of passion, as he tried vainly to get a serious discussion going about society and economic values, leapt out of his chair and sawing the air with his hands expatiated on our lethargy and lack of engagement, his slightly guttural, throaty pronunciation rendering it all the more emphatic: "What's wrong with you? When I was your age, I was a socialist. I was on fire with all the injustices in the world! I criticised the world around me. You are all asleep. Come on! Wake up!" This is a paraphrase but captures the spirit of the content closely.

The following chapters, then, will be a personal exploration of the shock waves that had me reeling and almost against the psychological ropes from 2015 to the present moment of writing. In a sense it is a small autobiography of a Jew coming to terms with these blows to the body that were a rather stern wake up call. A waking up to the trivialising of meaning, the crass emptying of language that hides the power bids, both individually and geo-politically, behind a welter of distortions and verbal games. For me, there was no clearer case of the abuse of language than the sudden appearance of wild and irrational charges of antisemitsm which were transparently aimed, often by non-Jews stirring up understandable latent anxieties within the Jewish communities, at those who were challenging the dominant orthodoxies of an economic system that had, since the late 70's created wealth inequalities not seen since the so-called 'Belle Epoque' of the late 19th Century. It must be emphasised that this is not a denial of antisemitism on the Left. As will be noted, it exists and needs to be challenged but a questioning of the use of antisemitism as a vehicle of political leverage that became part of a larger mechanism to undermine the Party of opposition and in particular its leader, an avowed anti-racist who had been active in this area for decades. This is the main purpose of this book: to raise questions about this narrative and for there to be another Jewish voice 'out there' that does so. I also incorporate elements of my own biography, in particular my own tussle with Judaism, from a religious as well as an identity perspective.

As I finish this introduction, I'm aware that I have already covered, in compressed form, many of the dominant issues that afflict our socio-economic life well before getting to the specific issue that will be the focus of this short book. I felt it was necessary to throw in the whole kit and caboodle at first so that the general scene could be set and seen in a more holistic light as things do not just emerge as isolated phenomena in political and social life, relating, as they do, to underlying trends and dynamics. The resemblance of this book's title, in inverted form, to the title of David Baddiel's book mentioned above, is, of course incidental but does, in this respect and on reflection, usefully serve to emphasise the mainstream media's and certain well know media figures' continual and unrelenting inversion of reality as a political tool. I will close this introduction with an example of Baddiel himself inverting reality, in a supposedly comedic context, some time before he wrote his titularly connected book. Baddiel, on Frankie Boyle's *New World Order* show, unwittingly strengthening the significance of the title of the show by rendering its ironic use literal, created a false imputation of an antisemitic conspiracy theory to a particular set of people on the Left by asserting that

> *'29% of Corbyn voters in the Labour Party think that the world is controlled by a secret global elite and that global elite are Jews.'[32]*

Baddiel was attempting to quote part of a Poll. The relevant question in the Poll that produced what was actually a 28% figure was whether the sample agreed that "the world was controlled by a secretive elite." No mention of Jews anywhere, of course. Given my own background, I am, of course, sensitive to the expression "secretive elite" because of antisemitic documents like the 'Protocols of the Elders of Zion,' a nineteenth century forgery that fuelled antisemitism and played a significant part in propaganda used by the Nazis. But there was absolutely no evidence that the statement referred to this nor any evidence that the respondents remotely had this in mind. Nor any evidence that the word 'elites,' as used in recent political discourse was generally referring to Jews rather than financial elites in general. Yet Baddiel bandied his interpretation around as if it were factual. By 2018, when Baddiel made this assertion, the political

---

32   https://jrschlosberg.medium.com/anti-semitism-among-corbyn-supporters-is-not-rife-and-the-bbcmust-broadcast-an-urgent-correction-55c3293393f2

atmosphere was already buzzing with dubious claims of antisemitism and the mainstream was gleefully running with what were largely smears, happy that they had, at last made something stick. This almost certainly strengthened Baddiel's ability to confidently make such a chutzpadik assertion. In recent years, critique of the financial establishment, whose reckless lending during the lucrative housing bubble that collapsed the world economy often referred to these institutions as the elite, the 1%, the 0.01% and there were rarely references to Jews except from Right Wing organisations and rarely the Left as Justin Schlossberg pointed out in his article on the Baddiel incident from 2018:

> *'So, for instance, more recent YouGov polling on anti-semitic attitudes among UK voters has shown that it is considerably lower among Labour voters compared to Tory, and that it has considerably declined since Corbyn became leader. But this, like the hard evidence of Corbyn's exemplary voting record on anti-semitism issues (and in contrast to most of his Parliamentary critics) simply don't fit the narrative that Baddiel and the BBC were exclusively promoting.* [33]

The fact that Baddiel could utter such a gross distortion with such ease and absence of compunction relied on the following factors:

1. A pre-existing mainstream media narrative that made groundless charges of antisemitism acceptable,

2. The manipulation of historically justified fears within the Jewish communities that gave these groundless fears currency.

3. The get out clause of *"I was only joking"* whilst knowingly adding fuel to a viciously skewed media scenario.

This is further evidence that Baddiel really knew that *'Jews did Count!'*

This short book, then, will examine various angles of the antisemitism issue combined with autobiographical input, the latter included to give personal context and as a therapeutic outlet after a torrid period where I was campaigning under the yolk of some trying health problems, trying to campaign as best I could within the parameters of these

---

33   Ibid.

limitations and supporting the Labour Party Parliamentary Candidate for my constituency in 2019. There was a lot of anger, let down and self-reproach to work through in the writing of this book; anger towards those voices of the official 'mainstream' part of the Jewish community (in reality communities) which tried to portray it as homogenous; anger towards what I saw as the desertion of a more radical tradition within Jewish thought; anger towards the way these official voices chimed in with establishment interests and anger towards myself for not being awake enough over the past four decades to absorb the reality around me. Had I been more conscious of this, I might not have been so constantly shocked and bewildered by the unfolding events. This book is, then, partly a personal archaeology, an exploration of a history I hadn't fully noticed and an appeal, in a period of almost grotesque conformism, for the true country that, in my sentimentalised way, I thought was the true homeland of Jews as mavericks: those, in the words of Heine, who dwelled in 'the portable homeland of the mind.'[34] Once again, this might sound savagely condescending coming from someone who is hardly an exemplar of excellence in the mental and cognitive spheres and whose life has barely manifested any degree of intellectual achievement, yet it remains there, for me, despite my own deficiencies, as a sort of ideal, that is hopefully more than a stale image in an era of stupefying acquiescence and bland assent.

Chapter One looks at some of the conceptual errors that are embedded in the leveraging of antisemitism in recent political scenarios in the U.K. It also specifically looks at how this use of antisemitism differs from its commonly understood meaning over centuries and how this is a dangerous force that militates in general against challenging all forms of racism. It also focuses on specific cases to illustrate how language framing has worked to shut down debate and create rigid stances that further discord, animosity and rupture within the Jewish communities themselves. Chapter Two looks further into language framing and uses textual analysis to show how a particular narrative can be furthered, not by facts but the creation of what I have called 'auras' based on the use of certain imagery as a propagandising tool alongside more egregious disinformation. Chapter Three delves into the evolution of this 'new' conception of antisemitism and its conflation of Jewishness with Zionism for geo-political purposes and how this evolved into an ethno-nationalist

---

34   Quoted in: M. Herbert Danziger, *Returning to Tradition*, p. 14.

form of Jewish identity, creating a much narrower concept of Jewishness but a concomitant widening net for potential antisemitism charges. This section also looks into the way in which the Labour Party, under Starmer, hard-wired the antisemitism narrative in order to create a fixed truth and a *Shibboleth* which would guarantee you a place in the Party as either a member or a prospective M.P. Chapter Four focuses on the utterances of two Chief Rabbis, one the current office holder and one his late predecessor and how they both chimed in with the dominant narrative in order to create forms of political intervention. In this chapter I have looked at the historical role that the Office of the Chief Rabbi has played and the way an artificial homogeneity has been imposed on the perception of the UK Jewish communities. Chapter Five, deals with the way manifestations of antisemitism are rigorously ignored as long as they do not contain anything pertaining to the geo-politics of the Middle East whilst anything critical of Israel is taken *prima facie* as antisemitism. I place this in the context of other forms of meaning that have been turned upside down using the metaphor of the *Mad Hatter's Tea Party* and the function of 'pastiche' as a postmodern phenomenon. Chapter Six is an exploration of identity with respect to identity politics and how the leverage of antisemitism is embedded in the new populism which exploits the need for psychological security through identarian politics which fans out through the various issues that have dominated UK and world politics in recent years. This is a highly complex area in itself and within the limited scope of this book is looked at largely from the point of view of Jewish ambiguity and insecurity around identity within the European tradition in contrast to its more recent hardening into armoured form.

The two Annexes are designed to bring out, by specific examples, the way both politics and social issues reveal a disturbing authoritarian component. The first is an analysis of an e-mail exchange between myself and a Jewish Labour Party M.P which shows how total control of the antisemitism narrative is demanded from M.P's so that they are mere functionaries who deliver utterances and statements according to a pre-prepared script. The second is a sort of reportage based on an encounter during the 2019 election campaign which revealed to me further that deeply disturbing changes had, indeed, taken place in British Society where disinformation, decoys and displacement are used to divert people from the underlying causes of their economic woes. In only the last few days, the obsessional focus on immigration, where people risking their lives in small boats are referred to as an 'invasion' and painted as criminals and delinquents despite the majority claiming asylum rather than being economic migrants, represents more distraction and displacement. The use of decoys and diversions such as this continues despite the causes of economic stresses such as unaffordable housing, low pay and collapsing services having zero connection to immigration, rather, being the result of a financial industry working a wealth extraction model.

This book does not attempt to deal with the political leveraging of antisemitism in UK politics in a comprehensive way. Many details and multifarious expressions of this phenomenon are not covered. To have covered every jot and tittle relating to this issue would have necessitated a much more voluminous product and taken up levels of energy that I simply do not have. I have, rather, selected certain features from the totality of events relating to this issue that seemed to me to bring into relief most clearly the nature and purpose of what was going on and continues to go on, in so far as this narrative remains intact. And it certainly seems to be the intention of the mainstream media and political establishment that it should remain intact as the mainstream media makes its final attempts to airbrush away the real history of the last seven years.

Chapter 1

A Label Becomes a Libel on the Wrong Lapel

The title of this chapter is an adaptation of a phrase used by Brian Klug[1] which I shortened slightly to emphasise it's inherent alliterative quality. It succinctly encapsulates what was starting to reveal itself in the post 2015 world of UK politics – that accusations of antisemitism were being applied loosely and prolifically. Towards the end of the Introduction I noted how David Baddiel's attribution of antisemitism to a belief about elites grafted on a meaning that was not inherent in the wording and was used as a form of libelling a whole group of people (in this case 28% of Corbyn supporters) in order to undermine a political movement. We also noted how, given the background buzz of dubious attributions of antisemitism for the previous three years the mainstream media had already created an 'aura' of acceptability that propped up the making of such unevidenced assertions with an attendant impunity. Klug's talk, given on the 75th Anniversary of Kristallnacht at the Berlin Jewish Museum from which my adapted chapter title is taken, asked some two years before the events in UK political life unleashed a wave of charges of 'antisemitsm' against the Labour Party, some serious and searching questions about definitions of the word and its legitimate application. It also pointed out the serious dangers of its misapplication:

> 'Antisemitism has rightly been called a 'monster'. But false accusations of antisemitism are monstrous too. For all these reasons and more, the word matters a great deal.'

---

1   https://www.jmberlin.de/sites/default/files/antisemitism-in-europe-today_2-klug. pdf p. 2

The 'reasons' why the use of the word 'antisemitism' matters, to which Klug refers, were enumerated in the preceding part of the paragraph:

1. '[B]ecause we want to develop social policies that reduce hostility to minorities, and so we need to try to pick apart different kinds of hostility: xenophobia, nationalism, anti-immigration sentiment, antisemitism and other forms of racism.'

2. '[B]ecause social statistics matter and we cannot have valid or reliable data about antisemitic incidents or antisemitic attitudes if we do not know what 'antisemitic' means.'

3. '[B]ecause it is heavy with history, echoing with the sound of shattering glass. As a result, it is not only a difficult word but a dangerous one, for it is a word that can do harm if it is misused.'

Yet, by 2016, the word was being bandied around by political commentators unanchored to any clear definition that could be of any value in aiding a discerning use of the term. One of the earliest manifestations of charges of antisemitism against anyone connected with the Labour Party were those levelled against the M.P. Naz Shah who posted an image already in circulation, of an Israel integrated into the map of the U.S as a new state, humorously intended as a solution to the Palestine/Israel conflict. Of course, Shah's posting, in 2014 before she became an M.P., had a far from humorous intention as it was posted as an angry response to the Israeli bombing of Gaza in that that year, a campaign that rained down what many saw as a grossly disproportionate level of destruction on the enclave, killing some 1,600 civilians including 550 children. The notion that someone sympathetic to the Palestinian cause should be able to express anger was not an unreasonable one. The disturbing issue and one germane to our discussion is: why was the manner of this expression of anger so quickly assumed to be antisemitic without any reasonable level of debate around the borders of meaning and applicability of the term and the context in which Shah's statements took place?

The Shah Facebook post was publicised by the Right Wing blogger known as Guido Fawkes, who, at this time, was to become a self-styled arbiter in what constituted antisemitism despite having no expertise or experience in that area. As we shall see, with regard to the mainstream media as well as bloggers like Fawkes, expertise was not a prerequisite, mere assertion was able to do the job. Within a short space of time, Naz

Shah had bowed down to the unofficial consensus that harsh criticism of Israel MUST be taken as antisemitism on face value with no debate or definitions involved. In an interview with Jamie Stern-Weiner, scholar Norman Finkelstein describes what he though Shah's media enforced *mea culpas* were actually about:

> *'They're making her pass through these rituals of public self-degradation, as she is forced to apologise once, twice, three times over for a tongue-in-cheek cartoon reposted from my website. And it's not yet over! Because now they say she's on a 'journey.' Of course, what they mean is, 'she's on a journey of self-revelation, and epiphany, to understanding the inner antisemite at the core of her being'. But do you know on what journey she's really on? She's on a journey to becoming an antisemite.'[2]*

The bizarre irony of the image having been posted from the website of a Jewish scholar who lost members of his family in the Holocaust and whose mother was a survivor of the Warsaw Ghetto should have fuelled a debate in itself had the feverish political, knee-jerk atmosphere not prevented it. A knee-jerk atmosphere that prevails today in a world collapsed into binary and excessively simplified descriptions that force us to live in caricatures. At the time all this emerged, I was dumbstruck by the sudden appearance of antisemitism as a hot issue. As I have noted, this was partly due to my lack of knowledge of the already potent historical evolution of the notion of what constituted antisemitism which I had thought was a specific term that referred to *hatred of Jews as Jews* and historically had indeed been such. The sudden heightened media concern for it in the UK and the accompanying *'philosemitism'* from non-Jews who seemed so exercised by antisemitsm, as if concerns for Jews had always glowed in their bosoms and was dear to their hearts, seemed suspicious and distinctly malodorous. This felt extraordinarily strange and artificial as there was little, historically, in the UK at least, that presaged such a concern, press coverage of antisemitism in the years leading up to 2015 being scanty to say the least. There was also the fact that *Jewishness* as an ethnic type identity had not been admitted to the BAME pantheon of

---

2   https://www.opendemocracy.net/en/opendemocracyuk/american-jewish-scholar-behind-labour-s-antisemitism-scanda/

admissible ethnicities. As a young man I had often bemoaned the fact that Jews, compared to other minorities, were never portrayed as 'cool' or 'trendy.' In the 80's and 90's, however, there had been a revival of interest in *Klezmer* music that largely emanated from Leftist New Yorkers and spilled over to the U.K which created interest and even a bit of trend setting.[3] But other than that Jews were barely considered a minority at all and almost an invisible entity as other groups asserted their ethnicity encouraged by a burgeoning identity culture. This identity culture became appropriated by neoliberalism with its emphasis on 'individuality' as opposed to the collective and a limited 'individuality' at that, defined only as someone who uses their agency via the wealth appropriation of the newly deregulated and unleashed financial institutions. 'Identity' was, in short, commoditised, so that whilst appearing a progressive stance, an industry developed around it that fitted in neatly with this individualistic economic ideology. This 'sidetracked' the emphasis from the economic and class sphere so that

> '[m]arginality is no longer described in terms of class but in terms of identity. Over the past three decades the struggle against...the capitalist class has given way to the struggles of a variety of (more or less) oppressed and marginalised groups: women, ethnic and racial minorities, the LGBTQ community, etc. As a result, class struggle has ceased to be seen as the path to liberation.'[4]

With the Klezmer revival and Left-leaning Jews in America reviving an interest in Yiddish there suddenly appeared a niche in the identity culture for those interested, who formed a particular community within themselves trying to revive some lost spirit of pre war, Jewish political activism. This was a fairly short lived phase with a fairly minority interest even within the Jewish communities. Baddiel's book about Jews not counting might have had some meaning forty years ago. And yet, after 2015, the 'community' seen as a monolith was suddenly centre stage with

3   https://www.klezmershack.com/articles/aboutklez.html
4   William Mitchell and Thomas Fazi, *Reclaiming the State, A Progressive Vision of Sovereignty for a Post-Neoliberal World*, p. 10. As I type these words, in the UK, there are signs of a resurgence of class consciousness after 40 years of its submersion via union leaders such as Mick Lynch of the RMT. Whether this presages anything substantive remains to be seen.

non-Jews pointing out alleged antisemitism as if they had suddenly become guardians of 'our' well being and safety. My initial surprise and shock quickly transformed into suspicion as I began, from the impoverished beginning of my awareness of the issues, to see that it was being used as a political tool both domestically and on the geo-political stage.

An examination of the Guido Fawkes report connected with Shah,[5] self-styled as an 'exclusive,' reveals certain trends in the framing of language which are clearly designed to enhance the resonances of 'antisemitism':

1. The word "transportation" is flagged up in inverted commas in the heading. A word with massively disturbing resonances for Jews since the Holocaust despite the fact that the original graphic, no doubt intended to be humorous, refers to the safety of Jews in a putative 51st State in America. It is clear that the dark resonances of the word have been exploited for full effect despite the lack of any underlying analogy.

2. In the body of the text, the word "solution" is emphasised in a way that makes it very likely the blogger was exploiting the horrific significance of the word. Again, the tongue in cheek graphic bears no analogous implications to those that the blogger's flagging up of the word "solution" are suggesting. This is the way Jewish fears were being shamelessly exploited for purely political reasons.

3. A photograph of Shah making a 'victory' sign at a pro-Palastinian demonstration which seems to be chosen for the similarity of the gesture to the *Hitlergruß*. This crude association was also used in a picture of Corbyn, where a raised arm movement was used in the context of creating auras of antisemitism by crude and utterly inappropriate allusions to Nazism.[6]

This creation of an 'aura' of antisemitism by emphasising certain words in order to create unjustified allusions was, as we shall see, a common go-to technique used during those years. This is more than ably demonstrated by the Labour M.P John Mann's response to the Shah incident which was so hyperbolic that it was off any measurable scale of decency and arguably amounts to a form of antisemitism itself in its abusive use

---

5   https://order-order.com/people/naz-shah/page/6

6   https://order-order.com/2019/05/17/hamas-salutes-jeremy-corbyn-solidarity-message-antisemitism-ridden-march/

of the Holocaust for purposes of political leverage. Mann, non-Jewish, who was to figure significantly in the use of questionable attributions of antisemitism during the succeeding years of the 'crisis', made a comment suggesting that Shah's words were reminiscent of Adolph Eichmann's plans for Jewish deportation. Of this use of the horrors of the Holocaust for political leverage, Norman Finkelstein stated that

> 'it ends up besmirching the victims of the Nazi holocaust, diverting from the real suffering of the Palestinian people, and poisoning relations between the Jewish and Muslim communities.'[7]

But Mann, later to become the Tories' *'Antisemitism Tsar'* (surely an offensive oxymoron itself!) felt free to do this.[8] This use of the Holocaust as a *ne plus ultra* of 'rug pulls,' immediately creating an incontestable and supposed moral high ground was to become a familiar feature of the 'antisemitism narrative' in the ensuing years.

About a week after Guido Fawke's 'exposé' of Shah's Facebook post from two years earlier, our 'antisemitism expert' unearthed a trio of posts by a Muslim Labour Councillor which he headlined as 'rants about "Jews."' Fawkes puts "Jews" in speech marks for some reason. Given that the comments make no specific reference to 'Jews in general' I can only assume that the speech marks were a subconscious admission that something was being 'stretched' by him here. The use of the word 'rant' and 'Jews' yet again exploits the Nazi era imagery of a prolix and ranting Hitler. Given that the posts quoted were very short and condensed expressions the noun 'rant' is hardly applicable given its definition in the Cambridge English Dictionary as *'a long, angry and confused speech.'* So the framing is rich in attributions and allusions from the start and it is worth looking at the statements in some detail to really focus on how a disturbing aura of antisemitism is created without due debate or examination.

The first post makes some sort of comparison between Israel and Second World War Nazis, referring to the 'genocide character' and 'arrogant mentality' that he believes Israel shares with them, pointing out

---

7   https://www.opendemocracy.net/en/opendemocracyuk/american-jewish-scholar-behind-labour-s-antisemitism-scanda/

8   https://www.opendemocracy.net/en/opendemocracyuk/american-jewish-scholar-behind-labour-s-antisemitism-scanda/

the 'irony' inherent in this. Any degree of comparison between Israel and the Nazis is taken *without question* to be antisemitism, yet we have on record Israeli Jews who have made this comparison regarding Zionists, some going as far back as the immediate post Independence period. Here is an extract from a letter sent by a man called Marcel who was, most likely, a North African Jew writing to a friend in Paris in 1949. The letter was stopped by the Israeli censor:

> *It's necessary to keep in mind that all of the Zionists are gangsters and even criminals. It is the country of antisemitism, without any exaggeration. All of the Jews of Europe have imported the totalitarian spirit of Nazism. There it is, my dear Ellie, the beautiful life of Ere[t]z [Israel]. It's too bad. The country doesn't lack attractions but because of these Hitlerites everything is under a shadow.*[9]

Even prior to the formation of the Israeli State, the Zionist oppression of the Yiddish language in order to replace it by the 'muscular' and 'clean' sounds of Modern Hebrew was compared with European antisemitism. One writer recounting the history of the *Hebraization* of the Eastern European Jews claimed

> *'[t]he new Jews, the Israeli, had to be the exact opposite of the old Jew. Zionism was at one with European antisemitism in rejecting the traditional Jewish image.'*[10]

Shlomo Sands recounts an episode, as a young student, when he felt a certain degree of shame in admitting he spoke Yiddish, such was the Zionist suppression of it as a symbol of the *'old Jew.'* The University English professor, tasked with improving the English of his students, asks them whether they spoke any second languages:

> *'...the teacher asked, 'Who is Shlomo Sand?' I raised a finger...'Sand is the only one to have mentioned Yiddish,' he said. 'Who else in the class speaks Yiddish?' Nine*

---

9   Shay Hazkami: *Dear Palestine, A Social History of the 1948 War*. I am grateful to @DonahueRogers for bring this to my attention.
10   Dovid Katz, *Words on Fire, The Unfinished Story of Yiddish*, p. 321.

hands went up. It was evident that, in the early 1970's, there were still many who dared not admit that they spoke the wretched 'language of exile.' To tell the truth, I was a little ashamed myself, and hesitated a while before noting Yiddish as a second language of mine.'[11]

In 1995, an Israeli professor of contemporary German history, Moshe Zimmerman, made the following remarks in an interview:

'It is obvious that we, from every aspect, have a better 'pretext' for many of our actions. Yet there is also a monster in each of us, and if we continue to assume that we are always justified, that monster can grow. Therefore, we Jews are obliged to always hold the German example before our eyes. Already today I am addressing a phenomenon which is growing: there is an entire sector in the Jewish public which I unhesitatingly define as a copy of the German Nazis. Look at the children of the Jewish Hebron settlers: they are exactly like the Hitler Youth...they think [of] themselves as the master race...'[12]

More recently, in 2016, Israel's deputy military chief, Major-General Yair Golan, stated in a speech given on Holocaust Memorial Day

"If there's something that frightens me about Holocaust remembrance it's the recognition of the revolting processes that occurred in Europe in general, and particularly in Germany, back then – 70, 80 and 90 years ago – and finding signs of them here among us today in 2016."[13]

Backtracking quickly followed by the Major-General but the above examples must surely question the knee jerk acceptance of such comparisons as inherently antisemitic. Yet the International Holocaust Remembrance Alliance (IHRA) 'working definition' of antisemitism

---

11   Shlomo Sand, *How I Stopped Being a Jew*, p.39
12   Quoted in: Gilbert Achar, *The Arabs and the Holocaust*, p. 234
13   https://www.reuters.com/article/uk-israel-holocaust-idUKKCN0XW0VF

includes, in its examples that follow what must be one of the haziest of attempts at defining antisemism that of *'drawing comparisons of contemporary Israeli policy to that of the Nazis.'* Yet, as we have seen, Jews have done that, including illustrious academics as well as a prominent member of the Israeli State's military hierarchy.

The second post from the councillor that Fawkes quotes and the only one to mention 'Jews' in some collective way, states that *'Jews in whose name Israel Zionist regime commit war crimes should worry it's same arrogant mentality as Nazis.'* The wording of this, again throws into relief how much definitions and intent matter in working out the boundaries of meaning around charges of antisemitism. The phrase *'Jews in whose name Israel Zionist regime commit war crimes..'* is somewhat ambiguous in that it could refer to ALL JEWS based on the notion that Israel is the 'representative Jew', a concept that has arguably been furthered by Israel's policies in recent years, particularly the Nation State Law. Or it could mean *those Jews* who identify with Israel and see Israel representing them, that is excluding non-Zionist Jews, anti-Zionist Jews and Jews who were simply indifferent to the whole thing. If the poster saw all Jews as represented by Israeli military policies thereby seeing Jews as a homogenous, Zionist entity then this would be indicative of the poster's ignorance of Jewish diversity and a possible form of unconscious antisemitism. If he had posted *'The Jews in whose name....'*, then overtones of antisemitism could well be argued, the addition of the definite article recalling it's use in the Gospel of John whose wording (οἱ Ἰουδαῖοι) is often seen as being the foundation of the tragedy of antisemitism during the last two millennia by seeing Jews as having some sort of collective responsibility.[14] But this is clearly not the case here. Fawkes, in his crude assertions lacking any nuance, the lack of which being the essential prerequisite for their political effect, does not invite us into any type of debate but claims immediate incontrovertibly. The insensitivity to language and framing determines everything. In one case, where Naz Shah, does, in fact use the collective noun *'The Jews'* and opens herself to the accusation of using a less disputable form of antisemitic language, it is quoted as if it had equal

---

14   It is worth noting here that the taken-for-granted 'antisemitism' of the Gospels and particularly the Gospel of John has been challenged by some theologians who see the language as referring to splits within different Jewish groups of the period where expressions like *'The Jews'* were referring to Jewish authorities of the time rather than 'all Jews.' See particularly: *The Parting of the Ways*, James Dunn, especially Ch. 8.

status with other locutions. Fawkes, in his whirlwind of *philosemitic*[15] concern for Jews is fuelling those binary simplicities which became the hallmark of British politics after 2010 in general, whether the issue was antisemitism, Brexit or the Welfare State. This strengthened the tendency toward polarisation and fostered a largely artificial culture war that, in my view, became forms of deflection, decoy and displacement that were about strengthening animosities and resentment. The politicised use of antisemitism functioned in a similar manner with the added danger, as Jewish scholars like David Graeber[16] have pointed out, that it was likely to increase antisemitism by creating blowback. Blowback tends to happen when political projects use blunt objects and have no awareness of the general dynamics within which they operate.

That education and light rather than heat are needed in this area by Jews, Muslims and the wider community is clear but it didn't happen because the dominant political forces regarded it as undesirable and preferred fostering polarisation as described above. It became an era of knee jerk, manipulative channelling of anger and the reinforcing of questionable allegiances whether to Israel or some sense of heart-warming nostalgia for a past where 'things were clear and simpler.' Nietzsche saw the philosopher as caught 'in the net of language' and it seemed as if the cynicism inherent in politics and mainstream media had suddenly discovered their longed for 'philosopher's stone' that opened the gates for endless manipulation of meaning, allowing them to abuse our chief mode of communication, rendering it a Punch and Judy show of stunted interactions that left people barking at each other while the housing bubble roared, proxy wars raged and wallets were handsomely lined.

It's worth touching on the issue of how accusations of antisemitism towards members of the Muslim community are used as if anger towards

---

15   I'm defining *Philosemitism* here as: a condescension towards Jews by the political establishment when that establishment, itself producing forms of antisemitism, 'pats Jews on the head' when they are useful for reinforcing their political and geo-political interests

16   See Graeber's prescient article: https://www.opendemocracy.net /en/ opendemocracyuk/first-time-my-life-im-frightened-be-jewish/, especially these lines: *'It is a campaign – which however it started, has been sustained primarily by people who are not themselves Jewish – so cynical and irresponsible that I genuinely believe it to be a form of antisemitism in itself. And it is a clear and present danger to Jewish people. To any of these politicians who may be reading this, I am begging you: if you really do care about Jews, please, stop this.'*

Jews, where generalised or specifically expressed towards Jewish Zionists by Muslims is subsumed under the same historic antisemitism that produced Nazism. This tendency ignores the specific historic and cultural context that has produced such anger and is, in part, generated by an aspect of Zionism that both wants Israel to be seen as *representing* all Jews whilst denouncing anger expressed towards '*the Jews*' being seen as an abstract collective as antisemitism rather than produced by the very identifications they foster. Stephen Beller outlines these issues:

> *Calling this hostility to current Israeli policies (which in any other context would be viewed as extreme nationalism), and towards the Jewish communities who are usually explicitly, and almost always implicitly, supporting these policies, 'antisemitism', or even the relatively recent 'new antisemitism' appears to me a deliberate attempt by Israel and its supporters to obfuscate the actual political and moral situation, and to smear Israel's opponents with the guilt of the Holocaust. Let us call these protests 'anti-Israeli', 'anti-Zionist', or even, at a stretch, 'anti-Jewish', but I do not think they have the same causation as historic antisemitism, and it is misleading to continue dragging this term in here.[17]*

Of course the appeal to *Jews* by the councillor (whether meant as those that consider themselves represented by Israel, or the more problematic *Jews* in general who are willy nilly represented by Israel as the voice of the collective Jew) that enjoins them to *worry* about the moral and ethical implications of the actions of Israel seems entirely reasonable just as any other members of a religious/ethnic group should be enjoined to examine questionable moral actions of any groups and individuals who appear to speak in the name of that ethnicity and/or religion. Again, a fruitful debate could have ensued that brought Jews and Muslims together but the peremptory adjudication of and tarring with the dreaded 'AS' word foreclosed such developments. Norman Finkelstein's view was that the Nazi comparison aspect of a statement such as the one under consideration was now of no further use even though, in the past

---

17   https://antonylerman.com/2014/08/04/anti-jewish-hostility-provoked-by-the-gaza-offensive-is-antisemitism-the-right-word-for-it/

'[i]f you invoked that analogy, it shook Jews, it jolted them enough, that at least you got their attention. I don't think it's necessary anymore, because Israel's crimes against the Palestinians now have an integrity of their own. They no longer have to be juxtaposed to, or against, the Nazi holocaust. Today, the Nazi analogy is gratuitous and a distraction.'[18]

As someone who went to school with many Muslims, who befriended Muslims, who played music with Muslim friends, who ate with Muslim friends, the missed opportunities for fruitful dialogue that could have taken place, had not the situation developed into crude and simplistic binary form fuelled by a powerful emotional charge, is, for me, deeply saddening. Much common ground could have been shared as

[t]he portrait of the Arab or Muslim sketched by contemporary xenophobia does not differ much from that of the Jew constructed by antisemitism in the early twentieth century. The beards, tefillin and kaftans of the Jewish immigrants from Eastern Europe at that time correspond to the beards and veils of the Muslims of today. In both cases, the religious, cultural, clothing and dietary habits of a minority are mobilised in order to construct the negative stereotype of a foreign body that cannot be assimilated into the national community. Judaism and Islam both function as negative metaphors of alterity; a century ago the Jew as painted by popular iconography inevitably had a hooked nose and sticking-out ears, just as Islam today is identified with the Burka, despite the fact that 99.99 percent of Muslim women living in Europe do not wear this full veil.[19]

The most saddening development, for me personally, was the quick evolution of the concept of the '*wrong sort of Jew.*' That is, those Jews who were challenging the accusations of antisemitism, seeing them largely as smears and the political leveraging of a historic tragedy which played on

---

18 https://www.opendemoc Enzo Traverso, racy.net/en/opendemocracyuk/american-jewish-scholar-behind-labour-s-antisemitism-scanda/

19 Enzo Traverso, *The End of Jewish Modernity*, p. 94.

the fears of a notionally united and homogenous community that, I was sadly discovering, was becoming institutionally more right wing, claiming often that Zionism equalled Judaism and chiming in with the populism that considered this Zionism a temporary ally. Nothing brought this out so clearly as when, in 2018, Jeremy Corbyn visited a *Passover Seder* held by a group called *Jewdas*. Not only does *Jewdas* challenge the mainstream institutions of the Jewish community that appear to prop up establishment interests but they clearly revel in an anarchic and surreal humour that is itself part of the phantasmagoric and often gleefully provocative traditions of Yiddish literature. In this respect, they are *more* connected to Jewish traditions than the mainstream institutions that arrogate to themselves the right to speak for British Jews. On their website, they invent a myth around their origins in a parodical parable of the discovery of an ancient manuscript written in a form of Yiddish predating Hebrew and teaching

> *'of the great radicalism of Jewish tradition, a tradition of dreamers, subversives, cosmopolitans and counter-culturalists. It waxes lyrical on the virtues of cosmopolitanism, putting loyalty to ideas of international justice over tribalism and parochialism, and attacks the oppressiveness of the 'natural' in favour of ethics designed to meet the face of the other. It preaches of the need to widen Judaism beyond the boundaries of those born Jewish, towards an ethic of wider concern, a Judaism that might at times stand in critique of the Jews. It prophesised a rise of 'international subversives' who would undermine power wherever they found themselves, who would preach veganism, pacifism and pickled cucumbers.'*[20]

Our redoubtable, self-appointed 'antisemitism Tzar', Fawkes, oblivious to any of the nuances of Jewish culture reported on this in predictable fashion,[21] stating that '[a]t the height of Labour's antisemitism scandal, Corbyn chose to mark Passover alongside a fringe group that despises and is despised by mainstream Jews.' By this time, of course, the so-called 'antisemitism crisis' bloggers like Fawkes, as well as the mainstream media,

---

20   https://www.jewdas.org/about/

21   See: https://order-order.com/tag/jewdas/

were assuming it was now an incontrovertibly accepted truth and 'done-deal' that could form the backdrop to any comment. *Jewdas* was described by Fawkes as 'unacceptable to mainstream Jews' which really meant only those subscribing to the views of mainstream Jewish institutions like the Board of Deputies whose representative status regarding what should be called *'Jewish Communities'* is highly questionable. This chimera of the 'mainstream Jew' had become a useful concept for those propagating the 'antisemitism crisis.' In reality it was a contradiction in terms. Jewish voices had always been varied and not easily assimilable to a monolithic image. But as we shall see later, there had been, for some decades, an attempt to imbue the Jewish communities with a univocal, monolithic quality which papered over the underlying elements of dissent and dispute. Fawkes' implicit dismissal of any other valid type of Jew than the putative 'mainstream' one could, arguably, be deemed antisemitic itself. Thus was created the bizarre and perhaps revealingly surreal scenario of mutual antisemitsm accusations being hurled at almost everyone in sight like a mud pie slinging fest which also occurred between opposing groups of Jews. Everyone is an antisemite except the real racists who had, temporarily, donned *philosemitic* masks trumpeting their newly-found Zionism alongside their racism creating the strangest bedfellows. The definition of antisemitism was clearly up for grabs and it was certainly being grabbed by the vested interest brigade with a vengeance.[22] Ironically, our *Philosemitic* exposer of antisemites, Paul Staines (Guido Fawkes) was not 'stain-free' when it came to mocking the Holocaust for juvenile political purposes whilst forging links with far-right, racist Parties like the B.N.P.[23] Such was Staines concern for the sensibilities of Jews back in his student days, that his creative outpourings included a ditty composed for the Federation of Conservative Students which went thus:

---

22 Norman Finkelstein has averred that defining antisemitism has always failed other than it's use as cover for Israeli State violence: *"It's been tried countless times before, and it's always proven futile. The only beneficiaries of such a mandate will be academic 'specialists' on antisemitism, who will receive hefty consultancy fees... and Israel, which will no longer be in the spotlight."* https://www.opendemocracy.net/en/opendemocracyuk/american-jewish-scholar-behind-labour-s-antisemitism-scanda/

23 brokenbottleboy.substack.com/p/disgusting-staines-guido-fawkes-is

FCS Bootboys

Gas them all,

Gas them all,

The Tribune Group trendies and all.

Crush Wedgewood Benn and make glue from his bones,

Burn the broad Left in their Middle Class homes.

No doubt Staines will have claimed 'youthful high spirits' for this ghastly concoction but it is, at the very least, indicative of how those who, it seems, couldn't care less about Jewish culture became staunch allies of a certain politically useful conception of Jews. The *philosemite* is, essentially, someone who is happy to pat Jewish people on the head as long as they fit into his/her geo-politics and economic ideology. Not playing the game is to be dismissed as the *wrong sort of Jew, a self-hating Jew, Kapo* and, of course antisemite. Thus Fawkes has no time for Jewish cultural traditions that lean Left, that include the great canvas of Yiddish literature with its visionary worlds and dreamscapes, that, like Kafka, left us with rich and stirring parables that created something unsettling, self-parodying and yet spiritually charged. In short the *philosemite* wants a parochial, Union Jack waving Jew who, as Cameron put it to the millstone-mortgage burdened citizenry, are '*doing the right thing*', or better put: are '*doing the Right thing.*'

As I read about *Jewdas* and the anarchic Seder, it all seemed to resonate with my somewhat romanticised image of Jewish Leftists and anarchists challenging the sweated Labour of *fin-de siecle* New York and *Bundists* challenging Zionism and their own communities without fear of being called antisemites or self-haters. I realised that I had grown up in a Jewish community which was largely shorn of such enriching traditions that would allow one to feel Jewish without necessarily being conventionally observant in religious practice. Perhaps my memories of my father shouting at Tories who appeared on the television was a sort of faint after-echo of this, a residue of this spirit. After spending years moving around the country rather incoherently, like a sort of psychological refugee, living in places where there were very few people of Jewish background I had, naturally, been distant from issues connected with the Jewish communities in the UK. Yet, despite these divagations, I still met isolated Jewish figures that were like little reminders to me of a sort of unstated community that defined itself, not by conventional identity but by a sort of anti-identity. In relation to this feeling of Jewishness as a sense of not belonging which no doubt merged with my own persona and sense of alienation, I found this relatively new ethno-national identity forged by Zionism utterly repellent and a denial of what made being Jewish enriching and challenging. Issues of identity and the complex subject of its attendant psychology will be discussed in a later chapter.

Holed up in my house in an isolated part of South West England. Walled in by M.E, O.C.D and a host of unnamed anxiety complexes, I felt far removed from the engaged world of political activists except for brief forays into the limited, local political scene. I could only largely observe from a distance like an invisible entity bewailing its lack of corporeality. That *Jewdas* existed was a reminder that this vital element of Jewish tradition remained and I wanted to delve into it albeit in my isolated, abstracted and almost virtual world. I bought books on Yiddish, a language I only knew through the handful of swear words and insults that remained in circulation: *Shmendrik, Shmok, Schlemiel, Schlamozel, Shiker, Mamzer* and *Tochas*. I bought a book of Yiddish invective so as to extend this limited vocabulary and on a more spiritually elevated level, read, slowly and painfully a volume of Yiddish poetry. Pronouncing it badly and relying on what remained of my memory of learning German and a bit of Russian, I stared at the script that breathed out the air of a distant and now lost world.

As a young man, I was conscious of feeling somewhat culturally and linguistically bereft and envied young members of the Asian community whom I encountered at school and who had been brought up speaking Hindi, Urdu, Gujurati, Punjabi, Sylheti and so forth. I idealised them, thinking that they were free from my dilemmas of identity and belonging and in my naivety failed to appreciate that, as time went on, young Asians were also starting to battle with cultural and identity issues of their own. Yet their access to an inherited language seemed to trump my sense of weaker cultural identity as I perceived it. After all, I was white and spoke with a Manchester accent. And yet I had memories infused with Jewish cantorial music and images of the flame-like lettering of the Masoretic Hebrew text and the sense of the centrality of Jewish cultural life within the European tradition. I had fantasied, as a young man, despite the almost total absence of any demonstrable academic prowess, that I somehow was entitled to be the heir of those *Mitteleuropa*, Jewish intellectuals, who 'included a great number of rootless revolutionaries, from Trotsky to Rosa Luxembourg, who made socialism their homeland and championed a universalist spirit above nationalist identities and borders.'[24] Only more recently and as I write these words, can I begin to appreciate that the very dilemma over identity and belonging was not only at the core of Jewish life over the last two thousand years but perhaps could be its greatest strength in the face of our now growing nationalistic chauvinism where politicians compete in flag waving exercises and millions of people rummage desperately through the detritus of their histories to extract from the refuse old rags and snatches, 'things of threads and patches' with which to hold floundering psyches together. I began to feel strangely grateful for this wake-up call with which the ghastly and cynical antisemitism smear industry had rudely aroused me, even though it was to wake me up to the realisation that what I thought was at the heart of the Jewish communities was largely lost - but not entirely.

---

24   Enzo Traverso: *The End of Jewish Modernity*, p. 22.

Chapter 2

Of Auras, Associations and Attributions

In 2017, Reporters Without Borders placed British press freedom in 40th place.[1] It's main concern was threats of legal action against whistleblowers, where it was perceived that 'national security' was threatened and increased powers given to security services in the surveillance of journalists. It also expressed concern over the general denigration of the press by those in power noting

> *'Donald Trump's rise to power in the United States and the Brexit campaign in the United Kingdom were marked by high-profile media bashing, a highly toxic anti-media discourse that drove the world into a new era of post-truth, disinformation and fake news.'*

There was, as far as I can discern[2], no reference to the disinformation bias in relation to the Leader of The Opposition in the UK nor the strange irony that it was the press itself, in its more populist form, that was propagating the media bashing as it formulated the 'culture war' between a so-called 'woke', liberal world and an honest-to-goodness, salt-of-the-earth 'ordinary Brit' who represented 'common sense' and the yeoman like solidity of the house-owner and millstone mortgage bearer. There seemed to be little concern expressed about the fact that it was the press itself in the UK, dominated by a handful of press barons, that was undermining '*the press.*' The largely right wing press in the UK was itself

---

1   https://rsf.org/en/worrying-moves-under-may-s-leadership-lead-dropped-uk-ranking-rsf-s-2017-world-press-freedom-index

2   The mysterious and conspiracy theory inducing *'sorry the page you are looking for cannot be found'* appeared whenever I searched for the RSF comments on the UK for that year!

the author of a profound disinformation machine that became one of the greatest manufacturers of decoys whose purpose was to aid the political establishment. The culture war decoy it created was analogous to the 'skivers versus strivers' furphy that created the first wave of mass hypnosis as the economy reeled in the wake of the banking crisis. What this period of time confirmed was a speeded up descent of journalism to a level that barely had the capacity to analyse, elucidate and educate. Rather, it was displaying propagandistic tendencies that promoted groupthink and knee jerk via the crude manipulation of emotion. The unprecedented daily vilifications of the Leader of the main opposition Party which after 2017, when the Labour Party nearly gained power and took away the sitting Government's majority, increased in vigour and force and should have shocked and rocked our media institutions with a public recoiling from this grotesque debasement. But this didn't remotely happen. There was very limited comment on the matter as if some sort of subconscious collusion between the public and the industry had been at work. A disturbing normalisation of these phenomena seemed to have fallen into place.

By the time of their report of 2022, Reporters Without Borders (RSF) stated the obvious, showing that this almost monolithic culture might well be a result of the concentrations of power connected with the press:

> 'The British media landscape has continued to face threats to pluralism. Three companies –News UK, Daily Mail Group and Reach– dominated the national newspaper market, concentrating power and influence in very few hands.'[3]

Only fringe media raised the issues of a grotesque democratic deficit in mainstream reporting. It was up to obscure websites, like this Canadian one, that spoke out about the issue, using an article that appeared in the London Economic, also a fringe, online publisher of political commentary:

> Ask ten people over thirty what they think of Jeremy Corbyn, and chances are you'll hear some pretty damning responses. But interestingly, most of the negative responses merely parrot headlines seen in the Mail, Sun, Express and Telegraph. You're hard pushed to hear something new.

---

3   RSF Website 2022.

> Corbyn hasn't even been safe from the 'bastion of
> independent journalism' the BBC. The London Economic
> reported news that one of Britain's leading barristers
> has evidence of BBC bias against Labour leader Jeremy
> Corbyn. Jolyon Maugham QC, director of the Good Law
> Project alleged that the BBC has indulged in showing
> "coded negative imagery" of Labour leader Jeremy
> Corbyn since his election in 2015. Even this week, BBC
> Panorama produced what is widely regarded as a
> hatchet job on Jeremy Corbyn and anti-Semitism within
> the Labour party.[4]

The descent of journalism towards being ciphers for establishment interests is not a new thing. One only needs to remind oneself of the Murdoch takeover of *The Times* in the early 80's which displayed "the manifestations of the same culture of too close a connection between one powerful media group and politicians" as Harold Evan's, a former editor of *The Times*, put it to the Leveson enquiry thirty years later.[5]

This race to the bottom into a spurious journalism that reflected establishment interests in the guise of 'reporting' was no more marked than in the case of the 'antisemitsm crisis' that relied on things becoming accepted as 'facts' that were nothing of the sort, instead playing a game based on images and associations. One of the most egregious cases of this and emblematic of the whole phenomenon was an article published in *Jewish News* written by Joe Glasman in 2018 which was at the height of the antisemitism accusations raining down largely on Corbyn, some Labour M.P's and a *putative* membership. Glasman is the head of so-called 'political investigations' for the charity known as *Campaign Against Antisemitism* (CAA). Whether the CAA, in its 'political investigations' was really engaged in a sort of agitprop which promulgated a particular, geo-political interpretation of antisemitism rather than real 'investigations' into a shared and accepted understanding of the word is certainly worthy of extensive debate. In fact the Charity Commission has regularly received complaints about the CAA from those concerned that the organisation had become explicitly political in its focus and was thus against the spirit and letter of the independence required for charitable status. In a predictable

---

4   canadiandimension.com/articles/view/jeremy-corbyn-is-the-most-smeared-politician-in-history

5   See: https://hackinginquiry.org/sir-harold-evans-murdochs-takeover-of-times-seminal-event-in-press-and-politicians-collusion/

and less than artful form of circularity, the CAA response to these criticisms was that they were, of course, de facto 'antisemitic.'[6]

Glasman's article for his blog in *Jewish News* carries the title *From Bistro to Bier Keller: Labour Antisemitism*.[7] The title, perhaps in similar vein to the title of this chapter, is a rather contrived attempt at alliterative wit yet containing an alarmist reference to the innocent bistro transmogrifying into Hitler and the *Munich Putsch*. So immediately we are in this hyperbolic world. Glasman's article has the air of someone smugly confident that what they are trying to say has been shown beyond doubt to be the case so that mere assertion and suggestion is all that is needed to add to the already existing skein of doubtful attributions. Already, in Parliament, as a response to Corbyn attacking the Government over the Windrush Scandal, the then Prime Minister, Theresa May, was ready with the decoy card of the antisemitism smear to deflect attention away from her Government's attempt at populist anti-immigration fear mongering. She asserted *'I will not take an accusation of callous from a man who allows anti-Semitism to run rife in his party.'*[8] So Glasman was already riding high in terms of how much of the creation of the aura of antisemitism around

---

6   In 2018 after concerns were raised about the CAA setting up a petition on Change.org less than artfully entitled: *Corbyn is an antisemite and must go*, a CAA spokesperson responded: *"The Charity Commission regularly receives complaints against us, most of which appear to be made by antisemites who object to our work."* See: https://www. civilsociety.co.uk/news/regulator-assessing-concerns-raised

7   https://blogs.timesofisrael.com/author/joe-glasman/?anchor=about-me

8   https://metro.co.uk/2018/04/18/theresa-may-accuses-jeremy-corbyn-letting-anti-semitism-run-rife-l labour-7478136/ Worth noting that in a debate on antisemitism that took place on the same day (April 17th 2018), Labour M.P, Graham Stringer, who represents a constituency in Manchester with substantial Jewish communities, both secular and Orthodox, stated the following: *'I represent one of the more significant Jewish populations in the country, in Kersal and Broughton, and I have worked with the Community Security Trust over a number of years to try to reduce the number of attacks on Jewish people in my constituency. I have to say that I have never come across anti-Semitism within my Labour party, and I have been shocked to realise that it exists in the party and among people associated with it. Does my hon. Friend agree that one of the things we can do to reassure the Jewish community, not just in my constituency but throughout the country, is to deal with any accusations through a **proper process** as quickly as possible and, where necessary, either throw the accusations out or throw the people out?* 'The debate, led by the then Home Secretary, Sajid Javid, referenced Jewish Labour M.P's Louise Ellman and Luciana Berger who were at the centre of antisemitism allegations against the Party as well as their local constituency parties. Their 'evidence' was taken on face value despite cursory glances below the surface revealing much unreliability. Clearly, there were never any **proper processes** in place for validating charges of antisemitism.

the Labour Party had formed a solid state of unassailable 'truth' based merely on repetition of an assertion devoid of any background facts.

Glasman begins his story by claiming that the experience he was about to recount gave him a *'glimpse into the future of British Jewry under a Labour Government.'* Yet Glasman then tells us he's talking about 'a minor incident' which he then relates took place after a Campaign Against Antisemitism rally in Parliament Square. Interestingly and revealingly, in relation to the thesis being expounded here, Glasman refers to the waving of *Union Jacks* as well as to the post-demonstration retiring to the pub which is described as something that *'Brits do'* as if there was a need to appeal to a conservative, populist framework, emphasising loyalty to the establishment, with him and his group exemplifying model citizens of populist Britain. I have already alluded to my growing awareness of and awakening to the conservative turn in the mainstream part of the Jewish communities that I found so unsettling and here, in Glasman's article, we can clearly see how it is manifesting in the expression of populist sentiment chiming in with Israel and Zionism's accession to the Pantheon, or, perhaps, the Pandemonium of populist and authoritarian governments. This confirmed my ever increasing awareness that much of the mainstream part of the Jewish communities and its institutions had become 'status quo people'[9] even as far as bolstering a Government that was becoming more and more anti-immigrant, repressive and antisemitic, but an antisemitism that was deemed 'acceptable' because the antisemites upheld certain geo-political interests that were favoured by these mainstream institutions.

Glasman's appropriation of the *language of ordinariness* which fits in with the Tory shift to populism, positing an abstract, normative, British citizen, a sort of *universal Yeoman* that could be appealed to as embodying the common sense of the chipper citizen who gratefully receives the pat on the head for 'doing the right thing,' is immediately striking. It struck me as deeply cloying and sycophantic in nature and reeking of the conformism that formed the basis of an arguably already existent proto-fascism. Glasman's world, depicted as the Arcadian tranquillity of politically neutral and pastoral innocents, is then disrupted by the entry of the dreaded, putative antisemite who very briefly walks into the scene as

---

9   See: Enzo Traverso, *The End of Jewish Modernity*, p. 55 et seq. Where this shift in the Jewish community towards conservatism and neoconservatism is discussed in an American and European context.

the disrupter of the normative world of archetypal *Brits*. "*I know what you lot do to the Palestinians*", the finger jabbing passer by says. Our crew of non-political *Brits* (one of whom happened to be wearing a T-shirt with a 'non-political' Star of David on it which only by chance bore a resemblance to the one on the Israeli flag) are nonplussed and taken aback that their innocent celebrations of Britishness could be so infringed. Glasman tells us that the rude man's comments forced them to be roughly 're-located' to the West Bank while they asserted their disconnection from such regions being mere *Brits* having a depoliticised pint as *Brits do*. Our crew of innocents then demanded to whom the "*you lot*" referred, to which the finger-wagger responded "*Israelis.*" Note: no mention of "The Jews" or anything remotely antisemitic but of course Glasman tries to get us to make the inference that Israel always equals "The Jews" and nor does he tell us that the finger-wagger might well have seen Israeli flags at the CAA demo thereby making the connection that the demo was not about common and garden antisemitism but also about Zionism. So we are left with the paradox that connecting Jews with Israel is antisemitic whilst the demonstration and the whole CAA campaign made a connection *with* Israel! Circular arguments are us, apparently when it comes to pinning this label on someone's lapel.

Glasman then digs himself in by linking the incident with childhood memories of being called a "fucking Yid" and "Jew boy" despite the fact nothing remotely like that was being said. We don't know whether the finger-wagger was the sort of person who would have said something like that, or felt something like that, yet Glasman is happy to bring this bit of mind reading in to play to develop a certain aura and attribution despite the lack of any clearly supporting evidence. Most revealingly, given the title of the blog post, is that *he doesn't even know whether the individual is a member of the Labour Party*! So the events taking place here have to be imbued with a certain meaning according to Glasman's clear agenda. Perhaps the most *chutzpadik* and circular of Glasman's assertions is that the rude finger-wagger was exemplifying the antisemitic trope that Jews were more loyal to a foreign power, than their own country when these particular Jews were exhibiting just that very thing by protesting with Israeli flags and a Star of David bearing T-shirt! In the end, Glassman, himself, after the 2019 election produced a whooping and gleeful paean[10]

---

10   https://www.youtube.com/watch?v=evSj4S4AC4Q

to this trope by celebrating the defeat of Labour, the only Party to offer the hope of change to a country ravaged by decades of neoliberalism, wealth siphoning, racism and the cruel scapegoating of the ill and vulnerable. What could be more damaging to Jews in general than the sight of a prominent Jewish person ostensibly claiming to represent the 'community' at large, displaying that economic injustice, raging inequality and environmental despoliation were acceptable to him as long as justice for Palestinians and critique of Israel were no longer mentioned? This is not to excuse any antisemitic responses to Glasman via the taking up of those tropes. Antisemitism as a response to anything a Jewish person may do is always wrong. And as Steve Cohen has pointed out so well, ascribing responsibility for that antisemitic response to a Jewish person is an act of false consciousness.[11] Tariq Ali was also wrong to say, in the wake of the 2021 Gaza bombings to suggest that attacks on Jews (such as those in London in the wake of the Gaza atrocities) would cease if attacks on Gaza stopped. Antisemitism is always the wrong response as is racism or anything that turns human beings into symbols. Glasman's crassness must be seen for what it is on a shared human level. I found Glasman's exultational ululations deeply worrying and as in the article previously cited by the late and great David Graeber, I felt like shouting *"stop it, please stop it – you are not helping Jews."*[12]

Glassman's peroration is no more than a pick and mix of events that, if represented as a statistic in terms of Labour membership figures, would barely register. He then makes everything about support for Israel using well worn cliches yet never mentioning that the relationship of Jews to Israel as a national entity is complex and nuanced. His references to *'muralgate'* are also inaccurate: the figures depicted were not all Jews (only two of the six, in fact) and Corbyn didn't 'back it' he merely asked a question about it with reference to Rockefeller, one of the non-Jewish financiers in the mural. As with so much else connected with charges of antisemitism, there was never any real debate about the mural and the figures it actually depicted and it was simply assumed to be antisemitic

---

11   Steve Cohen, *That's Funny, You don't Look Antisemitic*, pp. 130 et seq.

12   See David Graeber: https://www.opendemocracy.net/en/opendemocracyuk/first-time-my-life-im-frightened-be-jewish/ : 'And it is a clear and present danger to Jewish people. To any of these politicians who may be reading this, I am begging you: if you really do care about Jews, please, stop this.' Graeber was referring to non-Jewish politicians whom he saw as using antisemitism for political leverage. However, I think it is possible to see Glassman's whipping up of fear as part of a sort of symbiotic relationship with the non-Jewish politicians.

in intent.[13] Glasman knows he can get away with this level of inaccuracy because the previous three years had sanctioned it with the blessing of the media.

What we witness in Glassman's article is the extreme polarisation at work that creates an *'if-you-are-not-with-me-you're-against-me'* mentality that tried to represent the Jewish community as a united monolith and depict other Jewish voices such as non-Zionist, Left Wing Jews and non-Zionist Orthodox Jews as marginal people and even 'crazies.' Sociologist, Kieth Kahn-Harris has valiantly and movingly tried to call for a sort of détente between the differing factions whilst admitting that the divisions in the community had, by 2019, become almost irreparable.[14] This tendency to polarise, is, of course, a very obvious manifestation of our present social tensions as witnessed in the U.S which is often described as being in a state of civil war and in the 2019 UK elections which were dominated by the great 'decoy' of recent times, the Brexit versus Remain 'tournament.' The Brexit/Remain split, though, had a more or less 50/50 aspect to its divisions whilst the Jewish communities were dominated by a solid mainstream block pitted against a much smaller and highly vilified group of dissenters.[15] As a result of this, the dominant forces claim the minority sections of the Jewish Communities are 'fake Jews', 'self-hating Jews' or 'Kapos' and I have already mentioned in the introduction how

---

13   One could argue that because the images COULD be taken to be Jewish given the iconographic history that showed Jews as controlling world finance that even if the figures depicted were not Jewish there is an argument by iconography that it is an antisemitic image. This is an argument advanced by Bob Pitt which he delineates in his excellent and balanced article that details the complex issues surrounding the image that should have engendered a real debate rather than the knee jerk response that took place. Pitt makes it clear that Corbyn could not have been expected to know all the background to the image after one glance, his Facebook post focussing on Rockefeller, one of the non-Jews depicted in the mural: *'You really needed an understanding of Ockerman's Icke-inspired conspiracist ideology in order to grasp the antisemitic nature of his artwork. So it should hardly be a hanging matter that many of us, including Jeremy Corbyn, didn't initially get that. Of course, this didn't prevent Corbyn's political opponents from cynically hyping up an old and previously not very significant story in an attempt to damage the Labour Party and undermine his leadership.'* https://medium.com/@pitt_bob/antisemitism-the-brick-lane-mural-and-the-stitch-up-of-jeremy-corbyn-6656b77cc941

14   https://www.opendemocracy.net/en/opendemocracyuk/fear-being-bad-jew-response-david-graeber/

15   A simplistic extrapolation could be a ratio of 4:1 very roughly based on polls intended to indicate the percentage of the community that 'bought into' the antisemitism crisis narrative and those that didn't. The somewhat pejorative 'bought into' is here used consciously as indicative of the author's views.

these hideous terms were applied to me on social media in a way that was predictable and formulaic given social media's tendency to reinforce polarisation. Arguments like 'most Jews are Zionists' are often used to strengthen the notion that Judaism and Jewish identity is coterminous with Zionism with the 95% figure bandied around even though the polls that are used to back this assertion indicate nothing of the sort when their methodology is scrutinised.[16] Some, including myself, have tried to turn the tables on what 'we' see as an attempt to marginalise those Jews who disturb the monolithic image that the mainstream Jewish institutions project by asserting that the dismissal of the minority Jewish voice is, in itself, 'antisemitic.' At the very least it is contrary to the spirit of free speech and natural justice, to cite John Stuart Mill:

> *'If all mankind minus one, were of one opinion, and only one person were of the contrary opinion, mankind would be no more justified in silencing that one person, than he, if he had the power, would be justified in silencing mankind.'*[17]

Perhaps the *ne plus ultra* in the creation of auras, attributions and assertions of unexamined charges of antisemitism were those connected with former Labour M.P Ruth Smeeth. At this point we are dealing with a miasma of ill-defined and irrational statements that relied on a pre-existent and almost hallucinatory history of manufactured hysteria that was used as an established 'truth' on which the *Jenga* tower of further assertions could build the necessary manufactured consent.

The 'Smeeth affair', as is now well known, goes back to the launch of the *Chakraborty Report* into antisemitism in the Labour Party on 30th June 2016 which stated that the Labour Party 'is not overrun by anti-Semitism, Islamophobia, or other forms of racism.' At the launch, Marc Wadsworth, a seasoned anti-racist campaigner whose organisation, *The Anti Racist*

---

16   See: https://forward.com/opinion/430535/a-lot-more-jews-are-anti-zionists-than-you-think/ 'Firstly, asking about favorable views of Israel in some abstract sense is not especially instructive, as the term "Israel" can be adopted to refer to a wide range of meanings depending on how one chooses to use it. "Israel" can mean everything from the physical land and territory of Israel, separate from the political institutions currently governing it, to the creation of a new Israeli culture and the revival of Hebrew as a national spoken language, to the people Israel (Klal Yisrael) ourselves.'

17   Mill, *On Liberty*.

Alliance, had worked with Jewish barrister, Geoffrey Bindman, in drafting a Bill to make racial harassment and racial violence criminal offences, stated at this launch that he 'saw that the *Telegraph* [right wing U.K newspaper] handed a copy of a press release to Ruth Smeeth.' Marc Wadsworth added "we can see whose working hand in hand."[18] Wadsworth followed this with a comment about the lack of diversity in the audience, issues that had preoccupied him all his life. Smeeth is seen rolling her eyes and a man next to her is heard, just above a whisper, saying "antisemitism at an antisemitism inquiry." It turns out that the *'antisemitism whisperer'*[19] was an ex-senior correspondent of *The Sun*, another right wing tabloid that had immense influence. Within seconds one witnesses the unfurling of a smear recorded in real time – no debate, no discussion around definitions and boundaries of meaning, just another plugging of dubious attributions based on previously established narratives. It is worth noting that Smeeth ignores Wadsworth's following words regarding lack of diversity in the audience and there is and would be no attempt to talk to Wadsworth and find the common anti-racist ground that was really in everybody's interest on the Left. Of course Smeeth, herself, could barely be considered to be on the Left. Smeeth was too busy eye-rolling to even push back at the right wing 'antisemitism whisperer' sat next to her who could smell the enticing aromas of the emerging smear. The fact that two right wing journalists are associated with her at this event is, in itself revealing, indicative of how *'Jews Did Count'* as long as they were politically useful to the Right. And I include in 'The Right' the majority of the Labour Party that has, for decades, espoused neoliberalism, a profoundly right wing economic dogma.

In Septmber 2016, a mere three months later Smeeth, yet again, created auras, associations and attribution by vaunting victimhood statistics. She rolled out, very publicly, a round figure of 25,000 pieces of online abuse she had received. And again this dumper truck delivery was not questioned as to its content and origins but became yet another huge cloud within the miasma of media musings about Labour Party antisemitism- pure timing and association was enough to do the job.

---

18   The video of this incident can be viewed here: https://skwawkbox.org/2018/04/25/video-for-transparency-marcwadsworths-actual-words-re-ruth-smeeth/

19   On viewing the video, I could not help seeing a slight smirk on the face of the 'whisperer' perhaps an expression of glee as the next smear realised itself in front of him? I leave it up to the reader to decide!

'Oddly,' contemporaneous research into online abuse received by M.P's during that time period did not pick up anything like this mountainous mass of contumely:

> *Ms Smeeth claimed that she had received over 25,000 abusive tweets. This volume of online abuse was not picked up by three surveys that were undertaken at the time: one by the Community Security Trust, one by Salford University and one by Amnesty, all finding nothing like the volume of messages that she had reported.*
> *From the Salford study for example:*
>
> *In one of these prospective surveys, by Liam Mcloughlin and Stephen Ward of Salford University, on-line abuse was tracked for 573 MPs, for over 10 weeks from 14th November 2016 to 28th January 2017. Their results showed that MPs received a total of 4761 abusive tweets and that of the top 50, Corbyn and his supporting MPs had received more abuse than Labour MPs who had opposed him. In addition, those MPs who did not appear in the list of the top 50, including Smeeth, would have therefore received less than 50 abusive tweets over the whole 10 week period.*
>
> *With regard to the volume of messages Ms. Smeeth claims to have received, a Sheffield University study of abusive tweets in 2016 found that the highest number were directed at Jeremy Corbyn himself.*
>
> *In addition, no data appears to have been produced to show how many of these messages emanated from Labour Party members.*[20]

---

20 *Jewish Voice for Labour* media statement regarding the Jewish Labour Movement's submission to the Equalities and Human Rights Commission's 'inquiry' into the alleged Labour Party 'antisemitism issue.' https://www.jewishvoiceforlabour.org.uk/statement/jlm-evidence-to-ehrc-gossip-distortion-double-standards-and-presumed-guilt/

Yet another arch example of how easy it was to create great waves of disinformation when you are surfing a media machine designed to keep it all afloat. One could almost assert anything without it getting investigated with any modicum of thoroughness as long as it propped up the desired establishment narrative.

It's worth contrasting my own interpretation of these events at the release to the media of the *Chakraborty Report* with those of Dave Rich, an alumnus of the Birkbeck Institute for the Study of Antisemitism and a prominent institutional voice who propped up the notion of an antisemitism crisis in Labour. In his book he describes the incident thus:

> *'This direct attack on a Jewish M.P and the suggestion that she was conspiring with the media led to uproar. Shouts of 'how dare you' rang out while Smeeth left the room in tears. 'Antisemitism at the launch of an antisemitism report' Kevin Scholfield of Politics Home commented with some amazement as he watched the scene unfold.'[21]*

We are back in the Glasman world of bucolic innocents having their pastoral incorruptibility sullied by those dark forces. A world of clearly demarcated good and evil is sketched out here with no room for any genuine encounter. We can see what Rich is doing here with his framing: Wadsworth is not critiquing an M.P., rather a *Jewish* M.P. whose Jewishness is totally material to the matter at hand. What is being implied here? That a Jewish person cannot be critiqued even though what is being critiqued has nothing to do with them happening to be of a Jewish background? Wadsworth maintained afterwards that he had no knowledge of her being Jewish and even if he had, how would that have altered things – tip toeing around critique, or avoiding it entirely? It seems, then, that right wing dismissals of *Critical Race Theory* and the associated structural racism were suddenly revoked and rendered valid as long as they were exclusively applied to Jews when political leverage was required. Jews had suddenly risen to the top of the hierarchy of racism with whistles and bells attached[22] It looks as if *Jews did count*, and how!

---

21   D. Rich: *The Left's Jewish Problem. Jeremy Corbyn, Israel and Antisemitism.*

22   https://www.independent.co.uk/voices/critical-race-theory-racism-kemi-badenoch-black-history-month-bame-discrimination-b1227367.html

With no sense of reflexivity, Rich, in the lead up to the passage cited above, writes that the event 'took place at a volatile time in British politics' listing the EU referendum, the resignation of David Cameron and the turmoil surrounding the resignation of almost the entirety of the Shadow Cabinet and the rally of Corbyn supporters outside Parliament.' Yet he cannot see that he is playing his own roll in creating another polarity that is now so rigidly hard wired that the Jewish communities, divided by these issues can no longer talk to each other without vitriol. There are further issues to be discussed that emanate from these divisions and dividing walls: that it weakens the collective fight against all forms of racism. One of the most shocking developments for me was to witness many Jews continuing to support the Tories despite egregious antisemitism, Islamophobia and anti-immigrant stances that whipped up populist sentiment and in some cases defending it on social media because there was geo-political support for Zionism. Yet Kahn-Harris holds out some hope here:

> What I haven't given up hope on though, is the development of a form of anti-racism, and a Jewish engagement with it, that will challenge the division of the Jews into the good and bad variety.[23]

The Marc Wadsworth and subsequently the Chris Williamson case do not help us hold out much hope especially in a time of continuous polarisations over almost every issue: Brexit/Remain; Populism/Socialism; Climate crisis/Climate change denial and more of the same recently with the Ukraine crisis: Pro-Nato/Anti-Nato. Almost every issue becomes one in which it seems the psyche must preserve itself through staunch defence of its position.

The people tarred unjustly with the antisemitism brush often suffered afterwards both materially and psychologically. Marc Wadsworth has spoken about the devastating effect it had on himself and his family[24] especially as he went on to fight the libel case against the *Jewish Chronicle* a once reasonably respectable organ of the mainstream Jewish communities that, to date, has lost 4 libel cases (included the one brought by Wadsworth) and has been warned at least thirty three times by the Independent Press Standards Organisation for breaches of the Editors

---

23   Op. Cit.
24   See: https://www.youtube.com/watch?v=4V7vX8u56rQ

Code of Conduct. After winning the libel case against the Jewish Chronicle, Wadsworth affirmed:

> *"I am an ally of Jews, Palestinians and all other oppressed people and will defend my reputation as a lifelong anti-racist campaigner against any media that libels me, as I have done successfully in this instance. The witch hunt against the Labour left, accelerated by the current leadership, must be halted by any means necessary."*[25]

Wadsworth's moving cry *"I am an ally of Jews, Palestinians and all other oppressed people"* encapsulates the very thing that the weaponisation of antisemitsm was dismantling - the sense of being able to work together, collegiately, to fight racism in all its forms. It's worth noting here that the mainstream voice of a falsely monolithic image of UK Jews was far from oppressed, rather, it was very much in the driving seat with the media giving it a luxury sedan to ride in. Those Jews who were oppressed were the ones who challenged this mainstream narrative and its corruption of the meaning of antisemitism who were marginalised and vilified as 'fake Jews.'

On a very personal level, as I have already discussed, I struggled to comprehend what had happened to 'my' community to reach this point where charges of antisemitism could be used in such an imprecise and scattergun fashion or like some wildly out of control muck spreader. As I delved into this more I realised that something had happened to what I took to be a shared understanding of what antisemitism was. I grew up in a world where what constituted antisemitism felt reasonably clear and was not usually disputed, as Anthony Lerman describes it:

> *There have always been disagreements about the definition and use of the word antisemitism, but during the first three or four decades after the Second World War there was, broadly speaking, a common understanding of what constituted antisemitism. This linked it to the classical stereotyped images of 'the Jew' forged in Christendom, adopted and adapted by*

---

25 https://morningstaronline.co.uk/article/b/marc-wadsworth-wins-libel-case-against-jewish-chronicle

> *antisemitic political groups in the nineteenth century*
> *and further developed by race-theorists and the Nazis*
> *in the twentieth century.*[26]

As I started to look into this issue in greater detail, often gathering information from others on social media[27] who had an interest in these matters, I became aware, that in my rather naive, somnolent state and isolated from any Jewish communities, I had not followed one of the most important political developments in relation to Israel and the Jewish diaspora, that is, the transformation of *antisemitism* into the *New Antisemitism*. This use of crude accusations of antisemitism to undermine a movement that might have fostered the first real challenge to the depredations of neo-liberalism including sky-rocketing inequality; environmental and climate catastrophe; socially damaging debt and asset bubbles, might well have reached a point between 2015 and 2019 that should have required a revision of part of the declaration of the *London Conference on Combatting Antisemitism*. The declaration stated that there should be a firm intention to 'never again allow the institution of the international community to be abused for the purposes of trying to establish any legitimacy for antisemitism.'[28] Such was the gleeful confidence in the way the tragedy of antisemitism was abused for egregious political leverage by our major institutions that a *'never again allow'* declaration could indeed be very relevant in this respect as well. A further conference on the issue should have used such a clause to refer to the abuse of the meaning of antisemitism itself.

Jean-Paul Sartre, in his monograph on antisemitism, *'Antisemite and Jew,'* contrasts, a bit too simplistically at times perhaps, the rationality and analytical tendency within the Jewish character and its tendency towards a liberal universalism, against the irrationality of the antisemite who relies on an undefined 'intuition' combined with mystical and emotionally driven ideas:

---

26   https://www.opendemocracy.net/en/new-antisemitism/
27   I'm particularly indebted to @TweetForTheMany who pointed me in the right direction regarding the history of the so-called New Antisemitism.
28   https://www.jpost.com/jewish-world/jewish-news/declaration-to-fight-anti-semitism-signed-in-london

'The Jew demands proof for everything for everything that his[sic] adversary advances, because thus he proves himself. He[sic] distrusts intuition because it is not open to discussion and because, in consequence, it ends by separating men. If he reasons and disputes with his adversary, it is to establish the unity of intelligence. Before any debate he wishes agreement on the principles with which the disputants start; by means of this preliminary agreement he offers to construct a human order based on the universality of human nature.'[29]

It is as if, within this quagmire of ill-defined and highly irrational incriminations of antisemitism which were thrown around willy nilly, the voices of the mainstream Jewish institutions had abandoned the rational, the reasoned and the universal values Sartre sees as a feature of Jewish thought for a crabbed particularism that was closer to the irrationality and false consciousness of the antisemite who wants to be saved from 'the crushing responsibility of thinking for himself' as Sartre further describes the antisemitic type. Sartre's description of the antisemite uncannily describes those that now armed themselves with the weapons of smear and vilification in the form of the charge of antisemitism :

'The antisemites have the right to play. They even like to play with discourse for, by giving ridiculous reasons, they discredit the seriousness of their interlocutors. They delight in acting in bad faith, since they seek not to persuade by sound argument but to intimidate and disconcert. If you press them too closely, they will abruptly fall silent.'[30]

This bizarre inversion of roles seems to form part of an unsettling sense of things being turned upside down. It leaps out of a whole cultural history to form an irrational and rigid structure, creating a crude and simplistic idea of Jewish identity that mimics the vulgar stance of the antisemite. This, due to a concatenation of geo-political phenomena connected, as we have noted, to populism, Islamophobia and the temporary (for it is always

---

29   J. P..Sartre, *Antisemite and Jew*, Schoken Books, p. 114
30   Op. Cit. p. 20

temporary) *philosemitism* of the elites. But with this came a terrible loss: the desertion of Heine's 'portable homeland of the mind' and the drawing in of thought into a narrow space giving an easy sense of psychological security but evaporating away, by the heat of its irrationality, all that was truly valuable.

Chapter 3

The New Antisemitism, New-Old Labour and New-New Labour

In the Summer of 1990, after spending nearly a year studying at a *Yeshiva¹* in a largely Orthodox area of Jerusalem, close to the border with East Jerusalem, I prepared to return to Britain after finding my initial enthusiasm and desire to live an observant life was becoming harder to sustain as I plunged deeper into a depression, battling complex dynamics of emotional currents in a setting that was already riven with historical tensions. I was still outwardly observant: Keeping *Shabbat*, putting my *Teffilin²* on each morning and studying *Talmud*, yet wondering whether I could sustain this once back in England: would I really be able to walk around wearing a *Yarmulke*, keep going to *Shul³*, follow the rhythm and cycle of the fully observant Jewish year without the scaffolding of that culture around me? More importantly, did I really have the belief and faith – *Emunah*- to maintain it in a non-Jewish environment? I discussed the issue with another *Yeshiva Bocher (Yeshiva* student*)* who was also planning to return to the UK and he told me that it was a favourable time to feel comfortable affirming ones 'identity.' After all, multi-cultural Britain had become a place where all sorts of identities were now displayed freely and even celebrated: Asian *Melas⁴*; Gay Pride; Muslims wearing Shalwar Kameez; turbaned Sihks; dreadlocked Afro-Carribeans – so maybe my *knitted Yarmulke* would be able to join this rainbow coalition of identities.

---

1   https://en.wikipedia.org/wiki/Yeshiva
2   https://en.wikipedia.org/wiki/Tefillin
3   https://en.wikipedia.org/wiki/Synagogue
4   https://en.wikipedia.org/wiki/Mel%C4%81

I had never really thought of Jews having an identity in that sense. Jews didn't make a 'thing' about identity, did they? Wasn't the very notion of 'identity' a complex and ill defined thing where religion, ethnicity and the old fashioned term 'race' were blurry around the edges? Most significantly, Jews were white weren't they? Well, at least in Europe and America and they didn't come under the umbrella of the 'BAME' acronym. Yet here I was, being enjoined to see myself as part of the new identity culture. Despite all this, within a month of returning to the UK, I had sloughed off my religiosity, my knitted Yarmulke quickly left residing in a drawer, together with *Tefillin, Tsitsit*[5] and *Tallis*[6]. It was a bit like an actor leaving a role he had never fully grown into and quietly disrobing after their final, lukewarm performance.

By some seemingly strange form of synchronicity, there was, at this time (the early 90's), a revival of interest in *Klezmer*[7] music. This revival to which we have already referred, originated amongst largely left wing Jews in New York and was tied into a renewed interest in pre-war Jewish Socialist movements in Europe and America connected with *Der Bund*[8] and *Der Yiddischer Arbeters Ring*[9], the latter being a specifically American, Jewish socialist movement formed to support the new immigrant, working class communities. Suddenly something traditionally Jewish became almost trendy as bands sprung up with 'Lenin cap' wearing clarinettists with non-Jewish practitioners excelling in the form and conferring on it a multi-ethnic, universalist dimension as well as functioning as an intellectual commentary on American, Jewish social and cultural history.

So, had a post-modern sense of being Jewish arrived, leaving Jews with an 'identity' to hang their *Tevye* caps on? Well, maybe not quite. The revival of Yiddish and the progressive roots of many Jewish communities were largely created by a comfortably off middle class. The economic and social profile of the community had changed significantly as 'antisemitic barriers fell away after World War II and Jews rose to pre-eminence in the

---

5   https://en.wikipedia.org/wiki/Tzitzit

6   https://www.myjewishlearning.com/article/tallit-the-prayer-shawl/   (Tallis   is the Ashkenazic/Yiddish pronunciation – not to be confused with the great Tudor composer!).

7   https://www.iemj.org/en/klezmer-music-from-the-past-to-the-present/

8   https://en.wikipedia.org/wiki/General_Jewish_Labour_Bund

9   http://yiddish-sources.com/workmens-circle-arbeter-ring

United States'[10] as well as Europe. What I hadn't become aware of because for many years, I was not even looking, was how much Jewish identity had changed in recent decades and how my image of the universalist, socialist and maverick Jews challenging establishment interests had largely but not entirely morphed into something quite contrary to that. It was clear something had fundamentally shifted. Steven Beller explains this change in a straightforward way:

> *'The impact of Israel's existence on Jewish identity was relatively small to begin with but, over the decades, it has profoundly changed the situation of world Jewry.'[11]*

In his book, *The Holocaust Industry*, Norman Finkelstein, traces the post-war history of this transformation of identity, or, as we might put it: a transformation *into* identity. This process was intimately linked to the Cold War and the way in which the Holocaust was remembered, subdued or used politically. After the Second World War, the Left, with its internationalist/ Universalist leanings was being pushed into the background by a new Jewish 'mainstream' that was fearful of being identified as connected with 'Communism' or anything Left oriented so that:

> *'[w]ith the inception of the Cold War, mainstream Jewish organisations jumped into the fray. American Jewish elites "forgot" the Nazi Holocaust because Germany – West Germany by 1949 – became a crucial post-war American ally in its confrontation with the Soviet Union.'[12]*

This tension between the Left leaning, universalist tradition, so powerful in Europe before the war and an emerging mainstream voice representing a more settled, affluent constituency has, to varying extents always been present in American and European societies but the significant change in the post-war world was, as Finkelstein describes it elsewhere, that

---

10   Finkelstein: *The Holocaust Industry* p. 32 (Second edition).

11   Steven Beller: https://www.historytoday.com/archive/behind-times/antisemitism-socialism-fools

12   Finkelstein: Op. Cit. p. 14.

'domestically, as institutionalised antisemitism all but vanished and American Jews prospered, the bonds linking Jews to their erstwhile "natural" allies on the Left and among other discriminated-against minorities eroded.'[13]

Finkelstein points out that the mainstream Jewish institutions began to mirror the political and geo-political dominant stances of the establishment, at first suppressing the mention of the Holocaust (still on the lips of Left Wing Jews) in order to prop up the anti-Soviet tenor of the post-war period[14]. It was as if Jews, via their mainstream 'representatives' were losing their 'outsider' status.

This tension between a settled Jewish community not wanting to ruffle the feathers of the establishment and a more uppity, radical element has existed from the Enlightenment onwards. In Britain, this has manifested itself within the conflicts and difficulties that exist between the Chief Rabbis, Board of Deputies and differing Jewish communities, whether Orthodox or the politically active secular. As I will explore in the next chapter regarding the interventions of two Chief Rabbis in the so-called Labour 'antisemitism crisis', this has often involved issues around the identification of Judaism with Zionism where we get a sort of role reversal taking place after the1967, 'Six Day War' in the Middle East, at which point the Jewish mainstream becomes more vocally pro-Zionist:

'Everything changed with the June 1967 Arab-Israeli war: By virtually all accounts, it was only after this conflict that the Holocaust became a fixture in American Jewish life. The standard explanation of the transformation is that Israel's extreme isolation and vulnerability...revived memories of the Nazi extermination. In fact, this analysis misrepresents both the reality of Mideast power relations at the time

---

13   Finkelstein: *Beyond Chutzpah. On the Misuse of Antisemitism and the Abuse of History.* p. 27

14   See: Finkelstein, *The Holocaust Industry* p. 15 where Finkelstein describes the Anti Defamation League and the American Jewish Committee chiming in with McCarthyism, 'offering their files on alleged Jewish subversives to government agencies.'

and the nature of the evolving relationship between American Jewish elites and Israel.'[15]

Regarding the direction of travel in the Anglo-Jewish Community, it is possible to discern similar developments despite substantial cultural differences. A discussion that took place on the pages of the Jewish Quarterly in the 1950's about the extent to which Israel can be considered the representative entity for all Jews[16], is hardly conceivable now, despite there being a small but significant number of Jews that still raise this issue, such is the monolithic conflation of Jews with Israel/Zionism in papers such as the contemporary form of the *Jewish Chronicle* which played such a decisive and profoundly questionable role in the Labour antisemitism saga.[17] Particularly interesting is the turn towards the British Conservative Party which has, historically as well as very recently, evinced antisemitic leanings but fifty years ago it was the Party where 'suspicion, mistrust and the occasional dose of establishment Arabism and anti-Semitism were the norm.'[18] This uneasy relationship changed after 1979 with the election of Margaret Thatcher as leader, her election signalling

> *'a significant shift in both presentation and policy. Rhetorically, Thatcher espoused the virtue of 'Judeo Christian' values and built [a] strong relationship with the Chief Rabbi, Immanuel Jakobovits. The number of Jewish MPs on the Tory benches rose significantly to their highest ever number during her tenure, with many being promoted to high office during the Thatcher and Major Governments. At one stage more than a quarter of the Cabinet were Jewish MPs, and in Nigel Lawson*

---

15 Finkelstein Op. Cit. Pp. 16-17.

16 R. N. Carvalho: *Anglo Jewry and Israel. Jewish Quarterly* Vol. 5 1958.

17 To date, the Jewish Chronicle has received 33 rulings against it from the IPSO and lost four libel cases. A number of complainants requested that IPSO launch a 'formal standards investigation' but this was declined by the IPSO (https://pressgazette.co.uk/jewish-chronicle-faces-calls-to-be-first-subject-ipso-standards-investigation/). A statement from the complainants can be read here: https://twitter.com/JoBirdJoBird/status/1478665368977743873

18 https://fathomjournal.org/the-new-special-relationship-the-british-conservative-party-and-israel/ During the Labour Party antisemitism 'saga' there were egregious examples of traditional antisemitism within the Tory Party reported by but largely left to moulder silently by the MSM. The likely reasons for this are discussed later.

(Treasury), Leon Brittan and Michael Howard (Home Office) and Malcolm Rifkind (Foreign Office), the three great offices of state were held by Jewish MPs during these Conservative governments. Mrs Thatcher also offered steadfast support to Israel in contrast to her predecessor Ted Heath, who was perceived as taking the side of the Arab states during the Yom-Kippur War.'[19]

This rightward move at that time signalled the start of a process that has brought us to where we are today: a significant transformation from the politically aware community almost always in tension with its own mainstream institutions[20] that tended to back the prevailing establishment, to one which is almost fully aligned with those very mainstream bodies, where the politically engaged Left is seen as a marginal, almost '*un-Jewish*' rump. This journey to the Right has been accompanied by an arguable[21] transformation of the meaning and scope of antisemitism which is connected with geo-political changes, the centrality of Israel as a specifically Jewish State and the moving of the Holocaust into the geo-political arena.[22]

The fuller history of this transformation to the Right is laid out with considerable clarity in an *Open Democracy* article from 2013:

---

19 Barclay, A., Sobolewska, M., & Ford, R. (2019). Political realignment of British Jews: Testing competing explanations. Electoral Studies, 61. https://doi.org/10.1016/j.electstud.2019.102063

20 The late Marxist activist, immigration lawyer and campaigner, Steve Cohen, in his somewhat contradictory and paradoxically expressed but prescient book *That's Funny You don't Look Antisemitic*, described the relationship thus: 'Ever since the Jewish masses came here following the Tsarist pogroms, the British State has backed and encouraged an intermediate layer (in particular the self-proclaimed Board of Deputies) to control and de-politicise the community.'

21 I say 'arguable' because there are those that maintain there has been no shift in the meaning of the concept antisemitism and it is really one long continuity. However it is clearly possible to delineate a sort of 'crescendo' in the politicised use of antisemitism by the Right to leverage certain patterns of interest both in the respective domestic setting and on the world stage. As I argue, the events of 2015-2019 in the UK seem to have produced a *ne plus ultra*, parodistic level of this development.

22 Recent examples of this are Netanyahu's use of distortions of Holocaust history for politicised purposes. He has even been called a 'Holocaust revisionist.' Of course, the Holocaust can be 'leveraged' without necessarily indulging in revisionism.

'The British left's reflexive support for Israel gradually eroded from the late 1960s, and particularly following the 1973 war. At the same time, the Conservative Party, in thrall to the New Right, was coming to increasingly identify with Israel. Amongst the most pro-Israel of Tory MPs in this period, the historian William Rubinstein noted, were some of Britain's most right-wing politicians; including Rhodes Boyson, Julian Amery, Winston Churchill, John Biggs-Davidson (Chairman of the right-wing Monday Club) and Ian Paisley. In April 1979, the Jewish Chronicle quoted a 'prominent Conservative close to Mrs Thatcher' as saying: 'Conservatives, particularly those of the younger generation, admire the State of Israel for its independence and power. They see the Jewish State as a vital outpost of the free world in the Middle East...'

This period saw the establishment of Conservative Friends of Israel, which was set up by the right-wing religious Zionist and Conservative politician Michael Fidler. Described by his biographer as having had extreme political views 'reminiscent of the philosophy of Enoch Powell', Fidler favoured arming the police and restoring capital punishment, and campaigned to 'strictly enforce the Immigration Act'. Over 80 MPs joined his Conservative Friends of Israel group in 1974, including Margaret Thatcher, and within a year it had a larger membership than Labour Friends of Israel'[23]

The transformation of the use and boundaries of meaning of the concept of antisemitism that arose out of this transformation is generally referred to as *The New Antisemitism*. Due to my own lack of serious political engagement with these issues, for years consciously fleeing from anything connected with the Jewish communities, Zionism and Judaism, I had not come across this term before and had to read up about it, a period of history covering some 40 years. With complex phenomena like these

---

23   https://www.opendemocracy.net/en/opendemocracyuk/uks-pro-israel-lobby-in-context/

one ends up entering a labyrinth of contradictions, paradoxes, blurry definitions and seemingly irresolvable dilemmas that generate more heat than light. But an attempt at an understanding of this history of the transmogrification of the meaning and function of antisemitism in general discourse is important in order to make sense of how the antisemitism furore in the UK after 2015 was possible and enabled the Mad Hatter's Tea Party which it evolved into, where even the word 'banker' and critiques of capitalism were taken as antisemitic tropes.[24]

The literary starting gun for the evolution of the concept of a 'new antisemitism' was fired by the publication, in 1974, of a book with the very title *'The New Antisemitism.'*[25] Both authors were connected with *The Anti Defamation League*, an organisation, set up in 1913 and like the *American Jewish Committee* (founded in 1906), was established, initially, to help and support Jewish immigrants who were arriving in America largely from Eastern Europe and Russia. By 1974, the authors, National Director and Associate Director of the *Anti Defamation League*, presided over a well established and august institution with some political clout. The book acknowledges that in the post war years and more or less up to the time of its publication, antisemitism had declined significantly and there had been a 'honeymoon' period for about 30 years after the horrors of World War Two[26] and asks the question: 'is the pendulum swinging back? Is there a new antisemitism?'[27] Here, the notion of 'the new antisemitism' implies some sort of renewed onset of the 'old' or historically 'usual' form of antisemitism after an all too brief respite. Yet two pages later, the authors state that their 'task will involve, necessarily, some redefining of traditional notions of antisemitism'[28] and it is this latter 'redefining' that is really the heart of the matter and what, essentially, gives the game away. Indeed, we soon find that a major part of the authors' notion of redefinition includes,

---

24   For the 'banker' thing, see Tweet by Michael Rosen that refers to a previous Tweet by Stephen Pollard, former editor of the Jewish Chronicle: https://twitter.com/ michaelrosenyes/status/1110603502483636225?lang=bg Regarding the 'critique of capitalism' being seen as an antisemitic trope see: https://labourlist.org/2019/03/ siobhain-mcdonagh-links-anti-capitalism-to-antisemitism-in-labour/   Here   we witness the transformation of the historic tragedy of antisemitism into utter grotesquerie and pastiche.

25   Arnold foster and Benjamin Epstein: *The New Antisemitism*. 1974.

26   Ibid. p. 1

27   Ibid. p. 3

28   Ibid. p. 5

to a large extent, concerns around 'shifting gears on the Jews, particularly where Israel was concerned.'[29] And they state this despite the massively increased support for Israel by the U.S.A after the 1967 War:

> 'Then came the June war. Impressed by Israel's overwhelming display of force, the United States moved to incorporate it as a strategic asset...Military and economic assistance began to pour in as Israel turned into a proxy for US power in the Middle East.[30]

The book floats between examples of common and garden antisemitism, very much needing to be challenged of course and pointing out criticism of Israel/Zionism as if it were automatically and axiomatically in the same category. Even the authors themselves, when criticising those that question the ideology of Zionism, find it difficult to pinpoint the boundaries around the concept of antisemitism using havering phraseology such as 'approached the very edge of the line between insensitivity to Jewish feelings and anti-Semitism itself.'[31] One must commend the authors here for, at least, acknowledging this grey zone, except it is also a zone which is readily exploitable due its inherent lack of clarity and definition. Clearly, their 'redefining' lacked any real sense of being a definition. Fast forwarding to recent years in the UK political scene, it becomes clear how lack of clarity over definitions and boundaries of meaning could leave vast scope for crude political leverage. Thirty years after the publication of Foster and Epstein's seminal book Norman Finkelstein was able to write:

> 'What's currently called the new-antisemitism actually incorporates three main components:
>
> 1. Exaggeration and fabrication
>
> 2. Mislabelling legitimate criticism of Israeli policy.
>
> 3. The unjustified yet predictable spillover from criticism of Israel to Jews generally.[32]

---

29 Ibid. p. 16
30 N. Finkelstein: *The Holocaust Industry*, p. 20.
31 *The New Antisemitism*, p. 80.
32 N. Finkelstein: *Beyond Chutzpah*, p. 66.

Winding back thirty years from the above definition (with which no 'new-antisemitism' devotee would concur, of course), it is possible to see that Forster and Epstein's book does frequently meet the criteria mentioned above. For example, in the chapter where, quite rightly, the antisemitic utterances of a Puerto Rican school head is held up as antisemitism within the New York school system, Forster and Epstein relate how the racism and antisemitism of this *individual* was challenged by the head of the New York Board of Education, himself a Puerto Rican and veteran campaigner for Puerto Rican rights.[33] I italicised the word 'individual' to indicate how the events described by Foster and Epstein are often quite isolated in nature and in no way endemic to the society or institutions on the whole. Yet an aura is created that that might well be the case. We're back to auras and attributions once more.

At points in the book and prophetic for the future evolution of the 'New Antisemitism', the authors appear to use the charges of antisemitism as if they were a blunderbuss, the resultant scattershot hitting some of the most pacific targets including organisations and individuals highly sensitive to the historic suffering of Jews and bigotry in general. Most bizarrely and almost surreally, is the way the Quakers 'cop it' for merely expounding a more balanced view of the 1967 war in the Middle East which departed from the myths of a defenceless Israel about to be pushed into the sea by a coalition of Arab armies.[34] The famous Catholic peace activist, Father Daniel Berrigan also 'cops it' for having the temerity to suggest that Israel may be guilty of "domestic repression, deception, cruelty, militarism" and turning a "settler ethos" into an "imperial adventure" as well as creating "one and a half million refugees." Berrigan is quoted as saying were he a "conscientious Jew in Israel I would have to live as I was living in America; that is, in resistance against the state."[35] The utterly whitewashed view of Israel the authors put before us in their book clearly allows them to conflate critique of the State of Israel's actions as unambiguous antisemitism. Wind on forty five years and we have this raised to a general principal and a higher power.

---

33   *The New Antisemitism*, pp. 72-73

34   See: https://therealnews.com/nfinkelstein0601part1 The interviewer sums up the 'myth' that has been passed down to us by quoting from the New York Times on the 50th Anniversary of the war: *"This year marks half a century since the Arab-Israeli War of 1967 in which Israel defied annihilation by its Arab neighbors and also came to rule over Palestinian Arabs in captured areas, including in the old city."* Finkelstein responds: *"...what's wrong with it is it never happened, and that's usually a big problem. It's called "falsifying history."*

35   *The New Antisemitism*, pp. 88-89.

Another portent for the future present in Foster and Epstein's book is the representation of the Jewish community as a monolithic whole. Ironically (an overused adverb already in this book!), it is those that use this monolithic representation of "the Jews" that the authors, quite rightly, rebuke:

> 'one classic method of slurring Jews, is to generalise about Jews from the alleged specific characteristics or acts of some Jews that may or may not have anything to do with their Jewishness.'[36]

The *Anti Defamation League* and the *American Jewish Committee* both posit a monolithic view of what are, in reality, Jewish *communities*, where views on Zionism and Judaism vary greatly and arguably even more so in recent years.[37] As the authors point out, the antisemite uses the collective noun *"the Jews"* as a slur. However, the 'new antisemitism,' in more recent years, creates its own form of anti-Jewish slur by marginalising those Jewish people who do not subscribe to their notion of antisemitism and its link with Zionism. This, as we shall see, gave rise to the absurdity of the present leader of the Labour Party in the UK, Keith Starmer, ostensibly 'rooting out antisemitism' which process resulted in the suspensions of Left Wing Jews from the Party – the very Jews who are closest to the traditions of the *Bundists* and the traditions of standing for social justice. In the end Jews were over five more times likely to be suspended by the Labour Party under Starmer than other members.[38]

There are many other 'targets' for Foster and Epstein in their book. We'll look at them later when dealing with the elements of the recent bout of 'new antisemitism' in the UK as they reached peak absurdity. But the important point here is that Forster and Epstein set in motion a sort of 'business model' that twenty eight years later, Shulamit Aloni, former Israeli education minister could refer to as a 'trick we always play' in

---

36 Ibid. p. 106

37 Shifts are taking place, particularly amongst younger Jews with regard to Israel. See: https://www.rollingstone.com/culture/culture-commentary/israel-palestine-jewish-american-support-1172309/ In the UK, research carried out by the sociology department of the City University of London in 2015 (after the devastating Israeli attack on Gaza the year before) showed that personal identification as a 'Zionist' had declined by some 13% compared to similar research carried out by the Institute for Jewish Policy Research in 2010.

38 https://www.middleeasteye.net/news/uk-labour-antisemitism-accused-purging-jews-over-claims

response to a question about accusations of antisemitism against those that critique the policies of the Israeli state:

> *"Well, it's a trick, we always use it. When from Europe somebody is criticizing Israel, then we bring up the Holocaust. When in this country people are criticizing Israel, then they are anti-Semitic. And the organization is strong, and has a lot of money, and the ties between Israel and the American Jewish establishment are very strong and they are strong in this country, as you know. And they have power, which is okay. They are talented people and they have power and money, and the media and other things, and their attitude is "Israel, my country right or wrong," identification. And they are not ready to hear criticism. And it's very easy to blame people who criticize certain acts of the Israeli government as anti-Semitic, and to bring up the Holocaust, and the suffering of the Jewish people, and that is to justify everything we do to the Palestinians."[39]*

A veritable paper forest of books followed from Forster and Epstein's 'pioneering' work, mostly by future Directors of the *Anti Defamation League*. Ten years later, in 1984, Nathan Perlmutter's '*The Real Antisemitism in America*' was published and in 2010, Abraham Foxman produced '*Never Again. The Threat of The New Antisemitism.*' Norman Finkelstein asks, rather acerbically, whether or not this production line might not be producing certain benefits:

> *'The data on Antisemitism supplied by domestic American Jewish organisations such as ADL and the Simon Wiesenthal Centre...view Israel as their Mother land. And were they not able to conjure up anti-semitism, Abraham Foxman [National Director Emeritus of ADL] and Rabbi Hier of the Wiesenthal Centrer would face the prospect of finding real jobs. In the case of Foxman and Hier this would be a real tragedy: both get paid nearly*

---

39   https://www.scoop.co.nz/stories/PO1906/S00076/dont-be-caught-out-by-the-trick.htm

half a million dollars annually from their respective
"charitable" organisations.'[40]

At present, American historian, Daniel Pipes, keeps the flame of The New Antisemitism alive linking it closely with an anti-Left stance that Pipes might well have inherited from his historian father, Daniel Pipes, who evinced a strong anti-détente stance during the Cold War, at one point being upbraided by the U.S. establishment when he was quoted as saying, in a Reuters interview, that "Soviet leaders would have to choose between peacefully changing their Communist system in the direction followed by the West or going to war. There is no other alternative and it could go either way."[41] Forster and Epstein had also attacked the Left in their book[42] in a way that was to become all too familiar: critique of Western (largely US) Imperialism and its purported link with the dominant forms of Zionism[43] was considered as axiomatically antisemitic. This included the singling out of Left Wing Jews on the American political scene at the time which pre-echoes recent events in the UK which is the major focus of this book. The results of these developments have created, through their evolution over the last four decades, a situation where, as Professor David Feldman puts it, 'the overall effect will place the onus on Israel's critics to demonstrate they are not antisemitic.'[44]

---

40 Finkelstein: *Beyond Chutzpah*, p. 67.

41 https://www.nytimes.com/1981/03/19/world/us-repudiates-a-hard-line-aide.html

42 See: p. 125 et seq. *The New Antisemitism*.

43 I write 'dominant Zionism' because there were forms of Zionism that wanted security for Jews in Palestine but on a bi-national basis without the nationalism and 'maximalist' approach of the dominance of one group. These early movements that proclaimed a greater humanism, though still Eurocentric and arguably paternalistic in nature, offered a glimpse of a possible non-racist Zionism. Ahad HaAm, for example, saw the project as the establishment of a *'National Home for the Jewish People and not..the reconstruction of Palestine as the national Home.'* For an excellent survey of 'alternative; Zionisms see: I. F. Stone, *Underground to Palestine*, pp. 229-260 which includes the essays: *Confessions of a Jewish Dissident and The Other Zionism*. Needless to say, the precursors of what is now the 'dominant' from of Zionism, marginalised these more radically inclusive groups (I. F. Stone, ibid, p. 250). In the end, extremism from Zionist Nationalism and Arab Nationalists made real rapprochement impossible. (I. F. Stone, Ibid. p. 254).

44 David Feldman is director of the Pears Institute for the Study of Antisemitism, Birkbeck College University of London. Quoted in: Anthony Lerman: *Why Turning to Jewish Exceptionalism To Fight Antisemitism Is a Failing Project*. https://www.opendemocracy.net/en/opendemocracyuk/why-turning-to-jewish-exceptionalism-to-fight-antisemitism-is-failing-project/

Brian Klug sees this literature, where incidents of alleged antisemitism are heaped together (some unequivocal, others questionable and yet others absurd) as 'facts lumped together.' He goes on to say that 'while these facts give cause for serious concern, the idea they add up to a new kind of antisemitism is confused.'[45] Alan Dershowitz, states, quite brazenly, that Israel *is* 'the collective Jew,'[46] making the conflation of antisemitism with anti-Zionism complete. He and others create an essentialist notion of Zionism in relation to 'Jewishness' and Jewish identity which has brought with it disturbing and unsettling developments where alternative meanings, nuance and ambiguity have been abandoned. We are left with a polarised, corrupted and hegemonic hammer in a world that is making its way towards greater and greater division where 'intolerance of ambiguity'[47] has become an inherent feature of political discourse. This 'intolerance of ambiguity' and descent into authoritarianism is an egregious feature of utterances such as this from Abraham Foxman:

> *'anti-Zionism is not a politically legitimate point of view
> but rather an expression of bigotry and hatred.'[48]*

As has been mentioned earlier, we have witnessed the application of this blunt instrument in the UK political scene leading to the suspension and expulsion of non-Zionist Jews from the Labour Party as the Leader of the Opposition, Keir Starmer, hungry for establishment acceptance, began 'purges' of Left wing Jews as well as Left-leaning M.P.s who were being deselected for future candidature by 'trigger ballots' that were considered as having questionable integrity.[49] Implicitly, the New Antisemitism ordinances create a rigid concept of the 'good Jew' who is then appropriated into other geopolitical interests by 'philosemites.' In many cases the 'bad

---

45 Brian Klug: *The Myth of The New Antisemitism* https://www.thenation.com/article/archive/myth-new-anti-semitism/

46 Quoted in Klug. Ibid.

47 The expression *'intolerance of ambiguity'* was coined by the authors of a vast research project investigating and developing methodologies to measure and anticipate the formation of 'fascistic' character types. This research was published as: *The Authoritarian Personality*, Adorno, Frenkel-Brunswick, Levison, Sandford New York: Harper, 1950.

48 Quote in: Klug. Ibid

49 See: https://www.liverpoolecho.co.uk/news/liverpool-news/liverpool-labour-mp-ian-byrne-24604974 and: https://labourlist.org/2022/08/tarry-instructs-law-firm-over-allegations-of-irregularity-in-trigger-ballot-process/

Jews' even being shorn of their claim to Jewishness.[50] There is a rich and disturbing burlesque-like irony here, where Jews are 'harassed' for beliefs that don't conform to an authoritarian, hegemonic and politically leveraged notion of what constitutes the new antisemitism. And as Anthony Lerman has pointed out the anti-Zionism equals antisemitism argument drains the word antisemitism of any useful meaning:

> 'For it means that, to be an antisemite, it is sufficient to hold any view ranging from criticism of the policies of the Israeli government to denial that Israel has a right to exist, without having to subscribe to any of those things which historians have traditionally regarded as making up an antisemitic world view: hatred of Jews per se, belief in a worldwide conspiracy, belief that Jews generated communism and control capitalism, belief that Jews are racially inferior and so on.'[51]

The case of Diana Neslen, at the time an 82 year old Jewish member of the Labour Party, illustrates the *aporias* at work here. She had received a 'notice of investigation' from the Party centred around a Tweet from four years earlier in which she had affirmed '*the existence of the state of Israel is a racist endeavour and I am an antiracist Jew*.' Labour's use of the 'hegemonic hammer' was challenged on the basis that the holding of anti-Zionist beliefs were 'protected' under the Equalities Act of 2010.[52] Labour backed down immediately after they received this legal challenge but retreated behind a wall of silence, probably knowing that any court case would raze their antisemitism-narrative house of cards to the ground in a very public manner. Starmer himself said nothing, his policy of adopting

---

50 See: https://www.middleeasteye.net/news/uk-labour-starmer-israel-palestine-slammed-colonial-speech-bds. The notion that anti-Zionism equates with denying Jews self-determination is a staple of The New Antisemitism. This simplistic formulation ignores other forms of self-determination and self-realisation. Note Rivkah Brown's remarks in the article: "This is only true if one understands 'self-determination' as the right of a people to an ethnostate, an understanding I reject. In making this assertion, Starmer is trying to do what philosemites – who are simply antisemites who find a political use for Jews – have done throughout history: implicate Jews in their colonial project. I, like the rest of the Jewish left, will have no part of it.'

51 Lerman: Op. Cit.

52 https://www.theguardian.com/politics/2022/feb/07/labour-drops-case-against-jewish-woman-for-alleged-antisemitism

an intermittent Trappist ethos having been useful before in other areas such as the 'culture wars'.[53]

So, there we have it: another attempt at bolstering a distorted and simplistic notion of antisemitism thwarted, yet no ensuing debate, no real media interest, no reshaping of the campaign of smears that relied so heavily on corrupted concepts. This disabling of debate, as we have noted, such a feature of 'ambiguity intolerance' and the trashing of respect for educational values in themselves, is such a hallmark of our times, that one continuously worries where this is leading. The conflation of Anti-Zionism with Antisemitism was, effectively destroyed in this ruling which considered anti-Zionism a 'protected' belief and a belief that could properly be held by Jews as a feature of their sense of being part of a specific Jewish tradition. When Jeremy Corbyn mourned the death of his friend Uri Avnery, the Israeli peace activist and post-Zionist thinker, he posted this on Twitter:

> *'I'm very sad to hear of the death of my dear friend, Uri Avnery. He was a lovely man and an example to us all. Uri never relented in his pursuit of justice and for peace for the Palestinian and Israeli peoples. My thoughts are with his family and huge number of friends.'*[54]

Here, we have the basis of what could have been a real debate. Corbyn, by this time (2018) labelled a confirmed antisemite by the mainstream media, either directly or by implication, announced the death of Avnery in his penultimate Labour Conference just as the glow of 2017 was beginning to fade and the descent into the fateful polarisations and so-called culture wars of Brexit versus Remain[55] were to seal the fate of any hope of systemic change. Yet there he was commemorating a Jewish Israeli who fought in the '47-'48 war and whose concern for peace and justice brought him to write his book *'Israel Without Zionism'* in 1968[56]. Asking why there was so little interest in this would be the pertinent and of course rhetorical

53   https://www.newstatesman.com/politics/uk-politics/2021/05/keir-starmer-s-tactful-silence-culture-wars-won-t-lead-labour-victory

54   https://twitter.com/jeremycorbyn/status/1031525804344320001

55   For more discussion of this process of polarisation and its function as a decoy and displacement activity, see the *Postscript* to this book.

56   Uri Avnery, *Israel Without Zionism*, Collier Macmillan, 1968.

question. We are reminded, yet again, of the abandonment of 'the portable home of the mind.'

In his controversial and some times self-contradictory book on Left-Wing antisemitism[57], the late Steve Cohen, a radical anti-Zionist makes a vital point that there is a need to fully separate anti-Zionism from antisemitism. He states that this is 'the real political task- and one which should unite us all – [is] to separate them again.' Cohen makes it clear that there is no inherent connection between anti-Zionism and antisemitism telling us that

> 'it is not only absurd but reactionary to make a direct equation between anti-Zionism and antisemitism, on a theoretical level. The two are obviously not identical. Indeed, it is grossly insulting to define the struggle of the Palestinians for liberation as being in any way intrinsically antisemitic. It is similarly insulting to condemn as antisemitism any solidarity with that struggle. It is a tragedy there is not more solidarity – there cannot be enough.'

Cohen was writing this in the 80's as a self-confessed Marxist who wanted a 'no-State solution' in the Middle East (and implicitly for the whole planet!) and was talking about Left Wing anti-Zionism, on

---

57 Steve Cohen, *That's Funny, You Don't Look Antisemitic*. It was originally published in 1984 but reissued in a new addition in 2019 and unfortunately rather scandalously 'hijacked' and co-opted into the antisemitism smear campaign. The endorsement of Ruth Smeeth on the back cover is beyond any form of irony and gut-wrenchingly absurd. Smeeth, given her record, would have likely smeared Cohen the same way other Jews on the Left were smeared. Steve Cohen, in the view of this writer, would surely not have permitted such a pernicious misuse of his thesis if he were still with us. In my view, it was a gross act of disrespect to him that this present edition of his book was used to bolster the political leverage of antisemitism by the mainstream part of the Jewish communities. One of the original editors, Erica Burman, in a reappraisal of Cohen's book 36 years later, expressed her concern at the misuse of Cohen's text: *'As Steve put it: "There is no balance sheet with any form of racism" (p.16). That is, it was addressed to a debate occurring within British left and feminist movements. It was not written as a tool for the Right to beat the Left. Poor Steve (who died in 2009) might well have been horrified at its current use. Or more likely he would have felt vindicated in his anticipation of it being used as "perverse ammunition to reactionaries of all kinds, who want to denounce revolutionary change"'* (Burman: https://www.jewishvoiceforlabour.org.uk/article/reading-thats-funny-now-and-why-its-different-from-then/).

occasion and largely unconsciously drawing on antisemitic tropes such as 'world domination' or implying that Jews were responsible for creating antisemitism at times. He was critiquing elements on the Left in order to help clarify the situation *for* the Left. Steve Cohen, sadly, did not live to see the Corbyn years where anti-Zionism was crudely pushed as being coterminous with antisemitism for base manipulative purposes, yet his book, simply on the basis it included examples of Left antisemitism, was republished as if it were an ally in the smear campaign, conveniently ignoring Cohen's Marxists and thoroughly anti-Zionist stance. Yet another bizarre irony: his book was mobilised to prop up the abuse of the meaning of antisemitism, a narrative that would have certainly condemned Steve Cohen himself as a 'self-hating Jew.' As the saying goes, 'you couldn't make it up,' or, perhaps by now 'you could.' Erica Burman, one of the original editors of Cohen's book, points out this gross misinterpretation of Cohen's radical positioning which could not be further from that of the present day weaponisation of antisemitism:

> *'The context now is exactly the opposite. Then [1984], our political voice was rendered conditional on adopting an anti-Zionist position, an enforced and conditional predication that, we argued, was antisemitic in its presumptions (that is, presuming to tell us what we should think and say; discounting the specific Jewish history and relationship with Zionism, the State of Israel, as well as its actions towards Palestinians). Now, in contrast, it seems that anti-Zionist Jews are especially in the firing (or expulsion) line, and deemed especially culpable precisely as Jews. What is common to both cases, and is equally objectionable, is the demand that Jews uphold a specific, deemed 'correct', position because they are Jews, or in order to legitimately call themselves Jewish. This demand is antisemitic.'*[58]

Steve Cohen never subscribed to the New Antisemitism discourse, yet, unfortunately, his book, in its latest manifestation (2019) is being used as if it were part of that corrupted discourse, his text shorn of its nuances and radical insights, drained of its potency and left as a shrunken

---

[58] Burman: op. Cit.

husk to be used as firewood to advance the blaze of bad faith, distorted meanings and craven agendas.[59] We will return to Steve Cohen's radical insights later when considering issues of Jewish culture, identity and what has been arguably lost.[60]

The history of the New Antisemitism and its political potency is also reflected in the UN's repeal of *Resolution 3379*. This Resolution, passed in 1975, stated that the General Assembly 'determines that Zionism is a form of racism and racial discrimination.' It was repealed in 1991 with a rather muted statement that hid any hint of the political dynamics that led to it, as New York Times columnist Paul Lewis described at the time: 'The one-line resolution repealing the Zionism statement declared that the Assembly "decides to revoke the determination contained in its resolution 3379 of 10 November 1975."' It did not use the words "Zionism" or "racism" in the resolution.'[61] As Lewis points out in the same article, the political shifts behind this were, in fact, very clear, the vote reflecting 'the shifting political currents of recent years, the Persian Gulf war in particular, which split the Arab and Islamic worlds, and the changes in the former Soviet bloc, fostered by the collapse of Communism.'[62] Now, as I write these words thirty years later, more tectonic shifts are taking place, creating fresh geo-political alignments that are challenging the 'unipolar world' with who knows what consequences. But at the time, the 1975 UN Resolution marked the end of seeing Zionism as a Left leaning, progressive force and its revoking marked a significant shift. This opened the field to forcing a direct relationship between anti-Zionism and antisemitism. The metamorphosis from reasoned debate, shared understanding of what constituted antisemitism to the New Antisemitism position has been well described by Anthony Lerman and bears quoting in full here:

---

59   A personal note: I met Steve Cohen around the time his book was published and we even found ourselves sitting next to each other at a *Rosh Hashannah* (Jewish New Year) service which despite his professed atheism he had decided to attend. He gave me a copy of his book which I couldn't fully appreciate at the time due to my ambivalence in engaging with political issues beyond a general anti-Thatcher stance. It saddens me that his book is now being used to fuel forces he would have reviled. He struck me as a softly spoken, humble and generous hearted man still struggling with what it was to be Jewish and a radical progressive in his work as an immigration lawyer.

60   See the chapter entitled *"If You're an Antisemite, I'm a Jew."*

61   https://www.nytimes.com/1991/12/17/world/un-repeals-its-75-resolution-equating-zionism-with-racism.html

62   https://www.opendemocracy.net/en/new-antisemitism/

While some writers, academics and commentators were convinced from early on that Arab hostility to Zionism and Israel was antisemitic, during the 1970s and 1980s there was considerable debate and reasoned disagreement about the validity of the charge. Political and ideological considerations played a relatively small part in the growing numbers of conferences and seminars taking place to discuss the issue. But what began largely as a series of intellectual and academic discussions gradually changed character as pro-Israel advocacy groups, the World Zionist Organisation, multi-agenda major American Jewish organisations (such as the Anti-Defamation League and the American Jewish Committee) and Jewish communal organisations monitoring and combating antisemitism took up the matter. Mounting international criticism of Israel began to have a major impact on their work. What started organically, morphed into a planned campaign'[63]

To end this brief 'tour' of the New Antisemitism world it is worth considering specific dangers that it has created, not just for the Jewish communities, the mainstream elements of which arguably consider it as a protective edifice, but also for the general challenges to racism, bigotry, nationalism and wealth extracting economic ideologies that divide us so much. One of the most damaging aspects of this development has been the rise of what Anthony Lerman has called 'Jewish Exceptionalism'[64] where a sort of stand alone approach has developed aided by the dominant institutions of the mainstream, yet not fully representative voices who have 'benefited' from the symbiotic relationship of the rise of populism and the ostensible interests of this pro-Zionist mainstream. Some of these patterns link in with other aspects of the rightward shift in the UK and the rest of Europe. In his book, *Cracks in the Wall*[65], Ben White charts this shift to the Right in the US and Europe and the anxiety that organisations like British Israel Communications and Research Centre (BICOM) and the

---

63   Ibid.

64   Anthony   Lerman   https://www.opendemocracy.net/en/opendemocracyuk/why-turning-to-jewish-exceptionalism-to-fight-antisemitism-is-failing-project/

65   Ben White, Cracks in the Wall, ch. 4.

Labour Friends of Israel have in trying to portray Israel as 'progressive' whilst Israel itself was starting to align itself with nationalist and populist countries like Hungary, Poland and India who had strong anti-immigrant and Islamophobic stances. Indeed, in the UK, as the Tories became more overtly anti-migrant and Islamaphobic, there was a correspondingly proportionate growth in condescending philosemitism[66] and geo-politically aligned pro-Zionist stance. This has been echoed by Keir Starmer as he reformed Labour into 'New - New Labour' after a leadership contest that some have seen as riven with mockingly transparent mendacity[67].

I have tried to illustrate this rightward shift on the cover of this book by juxtaposing two images that create a sharp and dislocating contrast. The top one of working class, young, Jewish men in Manchester demonstrating against the rise of fascism in Spain, some of whom might well have been about to join the 'Jewish Brigade' in Spain to fight this fascism. One notes, in the clarity of their gaze, that they sense their cause is just and their values well defined. Below it we have the flyer for the Solidarity with Israel Rally of 2021 which was a rather limp and pale response to the vast crowds that responded in protest to the attacks on Gaza of that year. There we see the Israeli flag combined with the Union Jack, both, at this time, populist symbols of right wing nationalism, the Union Jacks showing the loyalty to the new post-Brexit world of vapid jingoism and the comfortable place Revisionist Zionism has within its framework. As we will explore later, the juxtaposition of these images summed up for me, perhaps in an excessively binary way, the extent of the transformation that had taken place. But what about the 'specific danger' referred to above? Well the pictures on the front of this book tells this story also: values that were considered universal such as social justice, fighting racism and bigotry have given way to a narrow particularism, the 'exceptionalism' described by Anthony Lerman mentioned earlier. This push to the right and the co-

---

66 Just a matter of days before writing this passage, Liz Truss, during her Tory leadership campaign, made a particularly inept statement while trying to woo the Jewish community as exemplifying Tory values, depicting them as defenders of the 'family unit' and 'starting up businesses': *"So many Jewish values are Conservative values and British values too, for example seeing the importance of family and always taking steps to protect the family unit; and the value of hard work and self-starting and setting up your own business."* This presentation of the community as a monolith using such crude, stereotyping terms exemplifies the stance of the condescending philosemite.

67 See: Aaron Bastani of Novara Media, https://novaramedia.com/2021/09/29/keir-starmer-is-just-as-dishonest-as-boris-johnson/

opting of mainstream Jewish institutions into the 'clash of civilisations' agenda of populism now makes this universalism nigh on impossible despite it being vital that all communities connect on this issue in order to resist these developments. In an article from 2015, Anthony Lerman ended on a somewhat bleak note:

> My pessimistic conclusion is that although there are still very many Jews who would actively sympathise with the aim of building an anti-racist political vision, the influence of 'new antisemitism' thinking, among other factors, makes it very difficult to see how what we understand as the organised Jewish 'community' could be persuaded to identify with such an enterprise.[68]

Three years later and three years into the extraordinary explosion of antisemitism accusations that were fired out like so much scattershot, rendering the term almost vacuous and a parody of itself, Lerman had harsh words to deliver to the official leadership of the pseudo-monolithic, 'Jewish community':

> Jewish leaders are struggling and failing to come to terms with new realities. They are choosing the utterly counterproductive path of isolation and exceptionalism, painting their community into a corner, making impossible demands for the eradication of anti-Semitism – which, like all racisms, can be fought and radically diminished, but will sadly always be with us – positively legitimising Jewish fears and doing nothing to discourage the narrative of exit one hears from family and friends as an answer to the insecurity Jewish leadership itself is exacerbating.
>
> Attacking the Labour party ...is just making matters worse. This is the time to take the path to working with other minority groups, civil society organizations and human rights bodies to confront antisemitism within the

---

68   https://www.opendemocracy.net/en/new-antisemitism/

*context of a wider antiracist struggle, not to perpetuate
the notion that Jews stand alone.[69]*

This dangerous 'sleepwalking' where narrow, apparent interests
are followed while the dangers of the bigger picture is lost out of sight
creates, also, specific dangers for Jews. In 2006, the late Jewish historian,
Tony Judt, pointed out the potential perils of voiding the meaning of the
concept of antisemitism, stating that 'genuine antisemitism may also
in time cease to be taken seriously, thanks to the Israel lobby's abuse
of the term.'[70] The New Antisemitism may well have created a dynamic
that has added to division, dissipation of energy and antagonism where
there should be debate, reconciliation and collegiality. At root, like all our
present polarisations and binary simplifications it may be the result of
not being able to face the demands of the unique features of the present.
Instead, as Enzo Traverso, has pointedly put it, 'when the insurmountable
traumas bequeathed by the past are projected onto the present, debate
slips into polemics that are both virulent and sterile.'[71]

---

69 https://www.opendemocracy.net/en/opendemocracyuk/why-turning-to-jewish-exceptionalism-to-fight-antisemitism-is-failing-project/
70 Quoted in: https://www.theguardian.com/books/2010/aug/08/tony-judt-obituary
71 Enzo Traverso, *The End of Jewish Modernity*, p. 83

Chapter 4

Two Chief Rabbis and a Damning

'Polemics that are both virulent and sterile'? That was about to be illustrated with neon lighting in the weeks leading up to the General Election of 2019 as an intervention from Chief Rabbi Ephraim Mirvis put the 'icing' on the 'New Antisemitism cake', 'over egging' the already overdone 'pudding' with a summatory flourish of all the landmark cliches that had accumulated since 2015. The hollowness and vapidity was so predictable that one would have been forgiven for believing that it had been written by a form of artificial intelligence whose software had been designed by a consortium of right wing philosemites in mainstream media together with the so-called 'official' representatives of what was fallaciously considered 'the Jewish community.' The crescendo of New Antisemitism madness had reached its effulgent apex. For Jews such as myself, it felt like the ultimate insult, the final vitriolic denigration of the Jewish values we held dear.

The ticker-tape of cliches ran thus: 'a poison sanctioned from the top'; 'I ask every person to vote with their conscience. Be in no doubt, the very soul of our nation is at stake'; 'the Jewish community has watched with incredulity'; 'we have endured quibbling and prevarication over whether the party should adopt the most widely accepted definition of antisemitism;' 'discrimination by the party against Jews has become an institutional problem.'[1] Mirvis claimed he wasn't telling people how to vote, yet he must have been aware of the significant support for the Tory

---

1   https://www.theguardian.com/politics/2019/nov/25/labour-has-let-poison-of-antisemitism-take-root-says-chief-rabbi

Party that already existed within the 'mainstream'[2] part of the Jewish communities making this assertion a mere rhetorical device designed, desperately, to preserve the illusion of political neutrality. Mirvis' assertions included some dubious information masquerading as facts, another characteristic of the whole saga of the antisemitism smears. He said there were '130 cases of antisemitism that were outstanding against Labour members' a number rejected by the Labour Party, yet even if the number were true they would be *claims of antisemitism only*, not cases of it! The language framing reveals the bad faith at work. Once more we see a flagrant abuse of language to prop up a politically loaded ideology. And let's be clear: in 2019 there were some 45 cases[3] of expulsion on grounds of alleged antisemitism, in numerical terms some 0.0075 percent of the near 600,000 strong membership.

As I became aware of this intervention that presented Jews in the UK in monolithic form by a clearly unrepresentative figure who belonged to an old institution whose claim of being 'representative' had been consistently challenged throughout its history, I registered yet another deep, resounding shock forming part of the multiplicity of shocks to which I referred in the introduction to this book. This shock was rather more specific in that I was reeling with disbelief that a Rabbi, the Chief

---

2   At the risk of putting nearly everything in single inverted commas, I use them here because the word 'mainstream' in relation to UK Jews is hard to define. There are mainstream institutions for sure, like the Board of Deputies, the Chief Rabbi's Office and the Campaign Against Antisemitism who set themselves up as arbiters of the concept of antisemitism as we have seen. But the real Jewish communities exhibit much more diversity than one would expect given the role these institutions have played in recent years. The left wing, radical and anarchist movement Jewdas, questions the reality of a mainstream, writing: *'The idea that there is a "mainstream Jewish community" is a fiction, promoted by a group of self-selecting individuals and institutions who have run out of ideas. There are approximately 300,000 Jews in Britain, with a huge diversity of religious and political ideas represented among them.'* (https:// www.theguardian.com/commentisfree/2018/apr/03/jeremy-corbyn-passover-jewdas-good-news).

3   See Andrew Feinstein's post on the Truth Defence blog: https:/truthdefence. org/thc-ehrc-report-is-neither-robust-nor-reliable-it-is-deeply-flawed%ef%bf%bc%ef%bf%bc/ His blog post makes it not only clear that there were very few cases of antisemitism (and we don't even know how many of them qualified as 'real' cases) but that there was an institutional cover up by the Equalities and Human Rights Commission (EHCR), an arguably politically skewed organisation, who did not consider solid evidence showing that the Labour leadership's office was being undermined. The recent release of the extensive Forde Report, that *did* consider that evidence shows how flawed the earlier EHRC Report actually was.

one, could utter such words so lacking in nuance and stating unexamined assertions as facts. This, ironically, seemed to be the very diametrically opposed form of thinking to that of the tradition of Jewish thought embodied in the *Talmud* where everything is examined, combed through, differing meanings extracted until some form of consensus achieved. It was as if, the Chief Rabbi, in politicising his thinking had become *un-Jewish* in that very thinking! He accused the Labour Party of 'quibbling' over the IHRA definition', yet isn't that what the Chief Rabbi *qua* Rabbi should have been doing himself if we were to work towards a clearer definition of antisemitism? In that respect, the Labour Party, before it finally capitulated to the hegemony of the IHRA, was being more *Talmudic* than he was! Like so much of the antisemitism crisis, reality was being turned on its head as it became a Mad Hatter's Tea Party yet again. The Chief Rabbi seemed to have jettisoned his *yarmulke* for a top hat priced ten shillings and sixpence. As the impact of this event coursed through me, I decided, that very evening of 25th November 2019, to 'pen' a letter to the Chief Rabbi. Not that I would do it expecting an answer as it was likely his electronic mail box was already full but in order to channel the ire and indignation that was gripping me and needed an outlet. Before writing it it I had to compose myself and allow the exasperation to settle in order to channel my thoughts. I wrote the following:

> *Dear Chief Rabbi,*
>
> *You have shamed your office today and rendered the Jewish people even more vulnerable to real antisemitism by reinforcing the fake, media-induced antisemitism that you recklessly impute to Jeremy Corbyn and the Labour Party.*
>
> *To interfere politically at this point in an election in a way that could affect the only party that could bring hope and social justice to this country is beyond contempt and renders you unfit for office.*

As a Jew* and a Labour Party supporter, I am proud to be part of a venture that I see as a continuity of so many of my Jewish forbears who have fought for social justice here and in Europe.

You talk about 'the soul of the nation being at stake' YET have you not noticed what has happened to that soul over the last nine years where:

1. The poor have been vilified

2. The ill have been attacked

3. The mentally ill have suffered

4. Inequality has soared.

5. Greed and financial rapaciousness has flourished

6. Austerity has been unnecessarily applied after a financial crisis brought about by an out of control finance sector that has benefited the wealthiest.

Where was YOUR voice about the nation's soul then? Yet you inveigh against a decent and honest man who, even now, maintains integrity in the face of manifest manipulation, deceit and digital sleight of hand from the Tories.

You have shamed your office, the justice loving tradition of the Jewish people and laid the grounds for future tensions in the most irresponsible way.

---

*   It's worth pointing out here, that the phrase "as a Jew" as used by those critical of Israel and the antisemitism narrative has been used, largely on social media, by those propping up the 'new antisemitism,' to indicate that a Jewish person is using their Jewish background to legitimise what they consider to be their 'antisemitism.' The phrase 'AsAJew,' used in this compressed form is thus another way of accusing a Jewish person of being 'self-hating' etc. In short, it's a handy way of devaluing and dehumanising in what has become a typically polarised scenario. For a discussion of this term, see: Kahn-Harris, *Uncivil War*, pp. 94-95. Needless to say, this writer was labelled in this manner on social media.

You seem to lack the acuity of intellect to even spot the most obvious use of this bogus antisemitism as a political weapon. Justin Schlossberg of the Media Reform Coalition called the antisemitism saga 'a disinformation paradigm' and made a detailed study of the issue. The great scholar, Norman Finkelstein, likewise, sees this as a purely politically motivated attack.

How dare you, amateurishly intervene in this, betraying the great Jewish scholarly tradition of intellectual and analytical acumen embodied in the Talmud and the exegetics of the Chumash.

With profound sadness and considerable disgust,

Simon Cohen

This was later posted on social media and although I was not on any of those platforms at that time, I was informed by a friend that it received over 80,000 viewings. Subsequently, it appeared on two Left Wing blogs[4]. So, to some degree, the channelling of my almost incandescent anger had achieved a very modest degree of success and created a little ripple. As in the motivation for writing this book, I wanted to raise my voice to show there were Jews 'out there' who said 'no' to this narrative. The intervention by Mirvis was amateurish, inept and thoroughly unrepresentative of the concerns of a significant number of Jews, largely those on the Left that tended to see the Office of the Chief Rabbi as a cipher for establishment interests. The *Haredi* (so-called 'Ultra Orthodox') who did not particularly recognise that office's authority to represent them and who constitute around 20% of the UK Jewish population largely abjured the Chief Rabbi's statement. The *Haredim,* represented by *United European Jews* (a body speaking for the Ultra-Orthodox Jews of Europe) produced a statement vigorously distancing themselves from the Chief Rabbi's utterances[5],

---

4   https://voxpoliticalonline.com/2019/11/27/unafraid-jews-respond-to-chief-rabbis-and-other-claims-that-they-fear-a-corbyn-labour-government/ and https://dorseteye.com/dear-chief-rabbiyou-have-shamed-your-office-today-and-rendered-the-jewish-people-even-more-vulnerable-to-real-antisemitism/

5   https://skwawkbox.org/2019/11/27/pan-european-jewish-organisation-sends-letter-of-support-to-corbyn/ This letter spells out in great clarity that the attack on Corbyn was of a 'political and ideological nature' going further than the letter from the Haredi, UK Orthodox Union the year before.

having made a similar statement just over a year before, in September 2018, similarly distancing themselves from the criticism levelled at Jeremy Corbyn by mainstream, Jewish institutions including the previous Chief Rabbi, Lord Sacks at the time. The statement of the *Haredim* also inveighed against the spreading of hysterical assertions that Jews were on the verge of leaving Britain in large numbers.[6] Interestingly and revealingly, the 'official' Jewish Press denied the authenticity of both letters, the Jewish Chronicle, soon having to back down on the first[7] and it's subsidiary, the Jewish News, issuing an ambiguous report on the second[8]. This attempt at discrediting (note the word '*deceived*' in single quotation marks) the authenticity of the Orthodox Union's response to interventions by a previous Chief Rabbi and the present office holder arguably chimed in with the mainstream policy of marginalising other Jewish groups who did not fit the falsified image of unity and the desire to present Jews as an homogenous entity[9]. This desire to project a false unity and the attempt to force it on an in reality diverse and divided range of communities within the Jewish population of the UK has been something that had, historically, always dogged and bedevilled the functionality of the office of Chief Rabbi in its role as a sort of link between the perceived community and the ruling establishment. Steve Cohen, perhaps, has given us the strongest possible expression of this concern from his Marxist perspective:

> '*Ever since the Jewish masses came here following the 1880's Tsarist Pogroms, the British State has backed and encouraged an intermediate layer (in particular*

---

6   The Jewish Chronicle describes the letter and questioned its representative nature on 12th September 2018.

7   Here, on the 17th September, the Jewish Chronicle accepts the letter is 'genuine': https://www.thejc.com/news/uk/charedi-jeremy-corbyn-labour-antisemitism-letter-signed-by-rabbis-1.469880

8   https://www.jewishnews.co.uk/123-charedi-leader-deceived-into-signing-pro-jeremy-corbyn-letter/

9   The attempt to present the 'Jewish communities' as a monolith was, ironically, a major ploy of traditional antisemitism. Daniel Levinson, writing as one of the researchers into fascism after WW2, a major part of which is devoted to a socio-psychological analysis of antisemitism, wrote: 'The fact that people make general statements about "the Jew", when the Jews are actually so heterogenous -belonging to every socio-economic class and represent every degree of assimilation- is vivid evidence of this irrationality. This striking contrast between Jews' actual complexity and their supposed homogeneity...' Adorno, Frenkel-Brunswick, Levinson, Sanford, *The Authoritarian Personality*, p. 57.

the self-proclaimed Board of Deputies) to control and depoliticise the community.'[10]

But the phrase of the Chief Rabbi that stuck in my craw the most and which I flagged up in my letter to him, was *'the very soul of our nation is at stake.'* The 0.0075% of *alleged* cases of antisemitism in the Labour Party membership in 2019 was the 'very soul of the nation' being at stake? On the ITV website[11], towards the end of the report on the Chief Rabbi's intervention, a segue into child poverty figures became an unintended illustration of how, in reality, the 'very soul of our country *is* at stake' and had been for many years and how the Chief Rabbi cheapened the phrase by solely rendering it significant in relation to the particularism of the mainstream Jewish community's political leverage of antisemitism. Suddenly departing from the subject of Labour and antisemitism it went into 'now for something completely different' mode, noting that '[e]lsewhere, research from the Resolution Foundation economic think-tank said child poverty could reach a high of 34% if the Tories win the election because its manifesto fails to change existing policy.' The use of the adverb 'elsewhere' as a switch to a new subject speaks for itself in this context. One could argue that it's not the place of the Chief Rabbi to engage in politics but in effect he ended up doing just that so why wasn't it possible for him to speak out about the issues of austerity, the vilification of the ill and poor and grotesque inequality as part of a specifically Jewish concern as it had been in the past? The Archbishop of Canterbury had done so if in a rather muted, sitting on the fence sort of way and critics of the office of Chief Rabbi have even likened the office to that of an Archbishop (in the pejorative sense that it was alien to Jewish tradition).[12] The very 'soul of our nation' had, indeed, gone to the dogs but it had nothing to do with alleged antsemitism.

Historically, there had always been considerable tension between the more orthodox communities and the Chief Rabbinate dating from the late 19th Century, just as there were between other sectors of the Jewish

---

10   Steve Cohen. http://you-dont-look-anti-semitic.blogspot.com/2007/01/socialism-anti-semitism-thatcherism.html?m=0

11   https://www.itv.com/news/2019-11-25/chief-rabbi-warns-soul-of-nation-is-at-stake-if-labour-wins-general-election

12   See: Meir Persoff, *Another Way, Another Time, Religious Inclusivism and the Sack's Chief Rabbinate*, p. 292.

communities, whether it be Left leaning Jews or Reform and Liberal. In his book discussing divisions and differing 'positions' within the Jewish communities in the UK, Keith Kahn-Harris enumerates as many as thirteen possible classifications![13] Trying to find unity here is clearly a tall order which is why all Chief Rabbis have faced dissension and continual controversy. As regards Zionism, Herman Adler, chief Rabbi from 1891 – 1911 and pre-Balfour, rejected it for a mixture of theological and socially adaptive reasons. Theological in the sense that he upheld the belief, still current within ultra-orthodox circles, that 'it was opposed to the teaching of Judaism to hasten the redemption which was to be in God's good time and was not to be brought about by man's 'precipitate action.'[14] And socially adaptive in that 'he wanted to stress the exclusive loyalty of British Jews to Britain, lest the position and political rights of Jews be weakened.' Adler's position at that time being almost the opposite of today where the strong expression of Zionism by holders of the office appears to shore up the image of 'loyalty' to the interests of the establishment as we noted in discussion of the image on the 'Solidarity with Israel' flyer on the cover of this book, where the Union Jack is embedded within the flurry of Israeli flags. In Adler's day, the dominant issue was the 'Anglicisation' of Jewish immigrants who encountered antisemitism from the Left as well as the more familiar Right, largely connected with worries about immigration which legislatively expressed itself in the 1905 Aliens Act which restricted the immigration of Eastern European Jews. Since Adler, the subsequent Chief Rabbis have been more unambiguously Zionist with the exception of Immanuel Jakobovits (Chief Rabbi from 1967-91). He was of a politically conservative strain but his relationship with Zionism, was, nevertheless, more muted and he was willing, at times, to voice quite fierce criticism of the Israeli State, causing some controversy in his last year in office by stating that the situation of the Palestinians was 'a stain on humanity' and '[we] cannot forever dominate a million-and-a-half Arabs, lord it over them. This blinkered attitude is self-destructive.'[15] Perhaps Jakobovits was himself not fully aware of the shift in permissible thinking that had taken place by the time he made those observations.

---

13 Keith Kahn-Harris, *Uncivil War*, p. 39.

14 See: Benjamin J. Elton, *Britain's Chief Rabbi's and the Religious Character of Anglo-Jewry, 1880-1970*, p. 96.

15 https://www.jta.org/archive/british-chief-rabbi-chastised-for-remarks-criticizing-israel

With the late Jonathon Sacks, however, support for Zionism was unequivocal. In the 2016 *Home Affairs Committee Report into Antisemitism in the UK*, his views on the relationship between Zionism and Judaism and implicitly between anti-Zionism and antisemitism were reproduced thus:

> *In an article for The Daily Telegraph in May, the Chief Rabbi criticised attempts by Labour members and activists to separate Zionism from Judaism as a faith, arguing that their claims are "fictional". In evidence to us, he stressed that "Zionism has been an integral part of Judaism from the dawn of our faith". He stated that "spelling out the right of the Jewish people to live within secure borders with self-determination in their own country, which they had been absent from for 2,000 years—that is what Zionism is".[16]*

The notion that 'Zionism has been an integral part of Judaism' is highly questionable and indeed has been questioned both on theological and political grounds. It makes no distinction between 'Zion' as a symbol of yearning for a spiritual home and the 19th Century movement, inspired by the nationalism of that era, which added the 'ism.' Conflating anti-Zionism with antisemitism is 'understandable', writes Brian Klug, explaining the immediacy of the appeal of formulations such as Sacks'. But only if a 'narrow logic' is followed:

> *It is, of course, understandable that many Jews find this logic compelling. There is a long and ignoble history of "Zionist" being used as a code word for "Jew," as when Communist Poland carried out "anti-Zionist" purges in 1968, expelling thousands of Jews from the country, or when the extreme right today uses the acronym ZOG (Zionist Occupied Government) to refer to the US government. Moreover, the Zionist movement arose as a reaction to the persecution of Jews. Since anti-Zionism is the opposite of Zionism, and since Zionism is a form of*

---

16   *House of Commons Home Affairs Committee Antisemitism in the UK* p. 12.

opposition to anti-Semitism, it seems to follow that an
anti-Zionist must be an anti-Semite.[17]

Klug goes on to say that drawing this inference is not valid, because:

[to] argue that hostility to Israel and hostility to Jews
are one and the same thing is to conflate the Jewish state
with the Jewish people. In fact, Israel is one thing, Jewry
another. Accordingly, anti-Zionism is one thing, anti-
Semitism another. They are separate. To say they are
separate is not to say that they are never connected. But
they are independent variables that can be connected in
different ways.[18]

In the same article, Klug questions whether the 'Jewish people, constitute a nation in the relevant sense, the sense in which the principle of self-determination applies.' He also raises the significant point that bears upon the use of the word 'nation' as if it were analogous to the modern meaning, for '[t]here was no pre-existing nation, not in the modern sense of the word, where both territory and language are already in place.' Note here, that '*in the modern sense*' needs to be emphasised before we are served up with handy maps of the Hasmonean kingdom c. 140 BC as if they bear any relationship to modern, nationalistic claims of statehood. Klug also reminds us that '[t]raditionally, the idea of the Jewish people was centred not on a state but on a book, the Torah, and the culture (or cultures) that developed around that book.' Interestingly, the Hebrew word for 'nation' is Ummah (אֻמָּה). The Arabic (أمة) is clearly a cognate that refers to a 'community' not a nation state in the modern sense. This entirely amateurish insertion of comparative linguistics on my part might well be questionable but it ties in with the idea that many *Haredim* have of the '*ummah*' as being defined by the divine insights of their holy book. The *Satmer Chassidim*, for example. echo the traditional view to which Klug refers:

'Judaism rejects 'Jewish' nationalism it's either Zionist
Nationalism or Judaism the two do not go together. It's

---

17   Brian Klug, *The Myth of the New Antisemitism*, in The Nation https://www.thenation.com/article/archive/myth-new-anti-semitism/

18   Ibid.

the Holy Torah that kept us alive thru (sic) the ages.
While so many powerful dynasties are gone. We had no
army or land. But we had the Holy Torah!'[19]

This rather long aside is by way of saying that Sack's picture, as represented in the Home Affairs Committee report is not a complete one and thereby tendentious. The report goes on to point out that many Jews do not consider themselves to be Zionists (as much as 41% according to research in 2015) but considers the use of the word 'Zionist' in a negative way to have antisemitic overtones. It also recommends '[for] the purposes of criminal or disciplinary investigations, use of the words 'Zionist' or 'Zio' in an accusatory or abusive context should be considered inflammatory and *potentially* antisemitic' whilst reserving the right to debate 'Zionism' as an ideology.' The word *'potentially'* (my highlighting) is, of course, carrying some weight here and the ensuing years were to show nuance and context were being eschewed in favour of a rigidity that increased as informed debate retreated and barely made its presence felt.

The late Lord Jonathon Sack's, Chief Rabbi from 1991-2013, was considered to be the most media savvy of Chief Rabbi's in recent times. His voice was often to be heard on radio in particular, often invited on to tackle the tough kernels of the moral questions of our time. His extraordinary fluency in speech that sounded like he had written and honed it beforehand was combined with a liquid and mellifluous tone edged with a certain push in the voice that conveyed his insights had been arduously wrung through an internal and somewhat agonising mangle producing furrowed brows and strained and pained facial expressions. As with his successor, whose intervention was to come roughly a year later, Sacks' intervention with its peremptory sermonising functioned as a litany of the mainstream interpretations of certain events that had been used to vilify Corbyn over the previous three years. Sacks classically illustrates the license given to him by the preceding forty years of the New Antisemitism and the previous three years of media monstering to hurl out the charge of 'a-n-t-i-s-e-m-i-t-e' as if it were the most reasoned of accusations: "[We] have an anti-Semite as the leader of the Labour Party

---

19   Taken from a Tweet published by 'Torah True Jews,' a Chassidic, anti-Zionist group who challenge the conflation of Zionism with Judaism. See: https://twitter.com/TorahJews/status/1454878735807750148

and her majesty's opposition"[20] Sacks tells us as if it were objective fact with no space for doubt which is both strange from a Jewish angle as well as it coming from a former philosophy student. As we noted with Mirvis, there was something distinctly un-Jewish about contested concepts being flung out as objective facts. Elsewhere he adds the already stale canard used to exhaustion by the mainstream media that Corbyn is a supporter of Terrorism as he has "given support to racists, terrorists and dealers of hate." Right from the get-go, this type of charge, initially in connection with the alleged meeting with I.R.A members was used as a device to discredit and nullify despite Corbyn having firmly denied such vilifications, stating "I didn't support the IRA. I don't support the IRA. What I want everywhere is a peace process."[21] As soon as Corbyn had become leader the smears started like greyhounds out of the blocks with the then Prime Minister, David Cameron, claiming Corbyn was "security-threatening, terrorist-sympathising and Britain-hating,"[22] a statement made under the capacious umbrella of parliamentary immunity. Of course, a conflation was taking place here (conflations abound!) as freelance journalist, Luke Davies put it: 'many critics may be conflating the party leader's views on British rule in Northern Ireland with sympathy for the IRA.'[23] By the time that Sacks intervened, these myths and smears had been so repeatedly broadcast by the mainstream media that they had the status of home truths that had largely become mental wallpaper, so Sacks, referring to Corbyn meeting with the political wing of Hamas, was adding to a towering heap of contumely that was already in existence, the addition of further layers being mere effortless routine.

Similar things apply to his meeting in 2015 with 'Backers of Hamas' about which the media went crazy despite there having been prior meetings with Hamas representatives by Labour M.P's, Liberal Democrat M.P's and EU MEP's[24]. The Times of Israel reported that 'Corbyn spoke to Daud Abdullah, Azzam Tamimi, Zaher Birawi, and Mohammed Sawalha at a seminar entitled "The politics of reconstruction in Gaza" in the House of

---

20 https://www.newstatesman.com/politics/2018/08/corbyn-s-zionist-remarks-were-most-offensive-enoch-powell-says-ex-chief-rabbi

21 https://www.independent.co.uk/news/uk/politics/jeremy-corbyn-labour-party-ira-violence-1994-general-election-a7761801.html

22 Ibid.

23 Ibid.

24 https://www.aljazeera.com/news/2009/3/15/british-mps-meet-hamas-leader

Lords in 2015.' Corbyn had made it clear that establishing a peace process meant talking to people whose means and even aims you did not agree with and he stated, about that meeting (and implicitly others)

> *"Does it mean I agree with Hamas and what it does? No. Does it mean I agree with Hezbollah and what they do? No. What it means is that I think to bring about a peace process, you have to talk to people with whom you may profoundly disagree."[25]*

It is also well known that leading Israeli establishment figures[26] have advocated talking to Hamas, who, according to a United States *Institute of Peace* Special Report had 'sent repeated signals that it is ready to begin a process of coexisting with Israel.'[27] So, with the Sacks intervention, as with Mirvis, we are again in a sloganised world devoid of all nuance and reasoned debate. With regard to Corbyn's meeting with representatives of Hamas, it is worth pointing out here, that the Palestinian- British Hamas sympathiser, Azam Tamimi has been very critical of Hamas' use of antisemitic tropes in its earlier Charter saying, in a *Jerusalem Post* interview, that

> *"[a]ll that nonsense about The Protocols of the Elders of Zion and conspiracy theories -all that rubbish will be out. It should have never been there in the first place."[28]*

There was clearly some space for dialogue here but, as elsewhere, binary oppositions were considered the best way of preserving the status quo.

Without a doubt, though, the *pièce de résistance* of myth propagation was the reference to the incident where Corbyn referred to *specific* Zionists who were giving the former Palestinian Authority Representative to the UK, Manuel Hassassian, a rather hard time, as 'lacking in irony.' This event was subjected to a sort of intentional Chinese whispers game that transformed it into an assault on *all Zionists* and by new antisemitism

---

25 https://www.channel4.com/news/jeremy-corbyn-i-wanted-hamas-to-be-part-of-the-debate

26 https://www.independent.co.uk/news/world/middle-east/it-s-time-for-israel-to-talk-to-hamas-says-former-mossad-head-10311651.html

27 See: Norman Finkelstein, *Gaza, an Inquest into its Martyrdom,* p. 31.

28 Gilbert Achar, *The Arabs and the Holocaust,* p. 238.

extension, into *'all Jews lack irony.'* If it wasn't so sadly consequential it would be almost farcical, the more so as Sacks' comments actually are illustrative of the very thing that, *ironically* Corbyn was pointing out! As Larry Derfner deftly put it in *The Forward* on the 4th September that year:

> *'He was referring to an exchange that had taken place recently at a conference on Gaza that he hosted in Parliament. One of the speakers there, Manuel Hassassian, the Palestinian ambassador to the U.K., reportedly said, "You know I'm reaching the conclusion that the Jews are the children of God, the only children of God and the Promised Land is being paid by God! I have started to believe this because nobody is stopping Israel building its messianic dream of Eretz Israel to the point I believe that maybe God is on their side." Clearly, he was not being serious; he was being ironic.*[29]

The mainstream media were immediately tripping over themselves to see who could be the first to produce utterly misleading clickbait headlines: The Jewish Chronicle did not disappoint with *'Zionists' have 'no sense of English irony,'* the Times also did its best with *'Jeremy Corbyn: Zionists in Britain just don't grasp irony.'* Soon it became another 'fixed truth' that Corbyn meant all Zionists and according to the implications of New Antisemitism, all Jews. The mainstream media knew what they were doing: *'Corbyn's rough but clean political rejoinder was distorted into a now infamous anti-Semitic slur by lifting it completely out of context.*[30] A classic demonstration of this is Melanie Phillips' bilious display of New Antisemitism orthodoxy in her 'evidence for the proposition' in the debate: *'Anti-Zionism is Antisemitism,'* where she exclaims, mockingly, after parading grossly tendentious and misleading examples of putative antisemitism designed to tar all Palestinians and associated pro-Palestinian campaigners: "and it's supposed to be we Jews who are lacking in irony." Ironically (sic), she actually refers, to Corbyn's words as

---

29 https://forward.com/opinion/409563/the-missing-information-that-exonerates-jeremy-corbyn/
30 Ibid.

referring to *two* Zionists (closer to the truth) before twisting it to fit the *myth-become-truth-through-repetition* slander.[31]

This scandalous, context free adjudication of 'antisemitism' has it's roots in an abuse of what is known as the 'Macpherson Principle.' This abuse of the principle was significantly encouraged by statements from the 2006 *All Parliamentary Inquiry into Antisemitism* chaired by Labour M.P. Dennis McShane who went on to publish a book on the subject three years later unsurprisingly and unoriginally titled *Globalising Hatred, The New Antisemitism*. The inquiry grounded the basis for adjudging an incident as antisemitic on the Macpherson Principle which states that 'any incident which is perceived to be racist by the victim or any other person' should be recorded and investigated by the police and other relevant state agencies.'[32] They reformulated this as: '[w]e conclude that it is the Jewish community itself that is best qualified to determine what does and does not constitute antisemitism.' Yet, as Paul Keleman points out:

> 'There is, in this formulation, a significant slippage from the usage proposed by Macpherson. He had recommended that allegations of racism...be treated by the police and other state agencies as constituting a prima facie case for being racist and that, therefore they should 'be reported, recorded and investigated with equal commitment.' A complaint of racial harassment or racial discrimination does not circumvent the need to prove the allegation.'[33]

Typically, the inquiry did not resolve any real issues surrounding what was and was not antisemitism and as Kelemen states, references to the monolithic 'Jewish community' was, 'in practice, those considered to be its spokespersons.' [34]

The result of all of this is a free floating use of antisemitism allegations based on mere assertion which reduces the tragic term, at times, to a piece

---

31 For the quoted remarks see the video (https://www.youtube.com/watch?v=K1VTt_THL4A) at 11.06'. Phillips' earlier reference to the two Zionists to whom Corbyn's remark was originally and only directed is at 3.04'.

32 See: Paul Kelemen, *The British Left and Zionism, History of a Divorce*, p. 187

33 Ibid.

34 Ibid.

of playground abuse. The factions weaponising and using these allegation were allowed to get away with this knowing that litigative responses would come up against the wall of 'opinion' as this part of the ruling in the case of *Tony Greenstein v. Campaign Against Antisemitism* shows:

> *'In context, the labelling of the Claimant as "antisemitic" would clearly be seen as the author's opinion of the Claimant and that the definition of anti-Semitism was itself a matter of argument and dispute.'* [35]

This analytical laxity, context-free assertion and profound lack of nuance reached it's thundering climax in the interventions of Sacks and Mirvis. That a man of Sacks' intellectual calibre could indulge in such laxity seems, initially, mystifying. Perhaps the words of eminent Jewish historian Geoffrey Alderman can give us an insight into this paradox. He writes that:

> *'Sacks is an enigma. On the academic level, he is without doubt the most accomplished holder of the office of the British Chief Rabbi. But, in many respects, he lacks perspicacity. And (among other things) any sense of the political. Palpably, moreover, he lacks the courage of his convictions.'* [36]

Alderman also remarks on the apparent durability of Sacks despite these short comings and general concerns about the relevancy of the office itself writing that Sacks

> *'and his office have developed over time close, and mutually beneficial, contacts with the non-Jewish world. The life peerage conferred on him in 2009 reflects and demonstrates his standing in the eyes of the establishment. He is now virtually untouchable.'* [37]

---

35   https://www.5rb.com/wp-content/uploads/2019/06/Greenstein-v-Campaign-Against-Antisemitism-2019-EWHC-281-QB-final.pdf

36   Alderman's foreword to: Meir Persoff, *Another Way Another Time, Religious Inclusivism and the Sacks Chief Rabbinate*, p. xii.

37   Op. Cit. p. xiii.

Alderman wrote these words in 2010. In 2019 he must have been exercised enough about the exploitation of antisemitism for political purposes in general and the vilification by those means of Jeremy Corbyn in particular, to make a short video statement saying that '[Corbyn] has gone out of his way to help the Jewish communities and Jewish interests in this country.'[38] Significantly, Alderman refers to 'Jewish communities'-no plyer of the monolith myth he! It is also worth noting here, that Alderman is not a figure of the Left. In some areas he seems to express rather traditional views and in others more radical and progressive. In general, leading Jewish academics have questioned the use of antisemitism as political leverage and have been at odds with the official representatives of what is known as the 'mainstream Jewish community.' In April 2018, over forty academics, many Jewish, signed a letter published in the Guardian (who many see as having played into the antisemitism narrative[39]) opposing the framing of the so-called 'debate' (it never was one, of course!).[40]

Certainly these two 'court Jews,'[41] as Rabbi David Goldberg once described the functionaries of the Office of the Chief Rabbi, contributed to the demise of the 'Corbyn Project' although in ways that would be hard to quantify. The wider community would probably pay very little attention to the utterances of a Chief Rabbi generally, yet the massive media exposure itself on top of the prior build up after 2015 would have rendered their voice significant. It's certainly a sad and unsettling episode that capped a process of a convergence of mainstream media, right-wing Labour Politicians and the unrepresentative officialdom of the Jewish establishment to undermine the most significant expression for the desire for a change in economic ideology and geo-politics in the UK since the late 70's launched it's 'laboratory experiment' of financialisation and wealth

---

38   https://www.youtube.com/watch?v=WOW2TvQbA8I The video was made by a group called 'Just Jews' who describe themselves as representing 'an alternative Jewish perspective to that offered by the mainstream media.'

39   Matt Kennard of Declassified lists the *Guardian* as well as more obvious right wing papers whom he considers to have contributed to Labour's 2019 defeat: 'The campaign to make sure he never made it into No 10 came from the usual suspects on the right such as the Sun and the *Telegraph*, but self-styled left publications like the *Guardian* and *New Statesman* were key to it as well.'

40   https://www.theguardian.com/politics/2018/apr/02/stop-jeremy-corbyns-trial-by-media-over-antisemitism

41   See: Meir Persoff, *Another Way Another Time, Religious Inclusivism and the Sacks Chief Rabbinate*, p. 149

siphoning whose results are more than apparent to us now, forty years later. The Office of the Chief Rabbi was always a questionable one as we have seen. Whether this Office has any further meaningful function after being brought into such disrepute remains to be revealed. The use of the Office to chime in with a politicised and skewed interpretation of the meaning of antisemitism in such a blatant manner should raise questions about the nature of this Office and if it is a valid form of representation of the varied stances of Jewish people in the UK. The pro-establishment propagation of the monolith-view which has dominated in recent years by holders of this Office does not bode well for the survival of an intellectually and morally enriching dialogue within the Jewish communities themselves despite their history of lively dissent and challenge to the *status quo.*

Chapter 5

Obvious Absurdities

I can remember, towards the end of my student years, there was a resurgence of interest in the writings of Herman Hesse as well as the philosophers Ouspensky and Gurdieff. It was as if the now dying embers of the alternative movements of the 60's and 70's had suddenly been reignited, albeit very briefly, as the neoliberal period was already taking hold. Hesse's novels were being read and one could see occasionally a student carrying around a copy of Gurdieff's *Beelzebub's Tales to His Grandson*. This was a brief re-awakening of an interest in spiritual values just as the neo-liberal machine was to turn the housing bubble into a new theocracy before which the next four decades would offer their *Pujas*. Ouspensky was to Gurdieff as Plato had been to his teacher Socrates. In his book '*In Search of the Miraculous*,' Ouspensky recounts a memory of reading a children's book called '*Obvious Absurdities*,' the title of which reminded him of the way Western society had lost real spiritual values, creating a way of living that turned people into quasi-machines with only limited self-awareness and a society that was inimical to real human needs and growth. Reflecting on this as the developed world slid into the insensate barbarisms of the First World War could only have strengthened that observation.

Thinking about the Mad Hatter world of British politics where meanings become upside down and politicians speak with knowing smirks and tongues of a thousand tines; and how the cynical manipulation of antisemitism was used for cheap, political leverage. I, myself, recalled Ouspensky's recollection in turn, remembering that book of his I had read some years ago. He tells us that the phrase '*obvious absurdities*'

> *refers to a little book I had as a child. The book was called 'Obvious Absurdities,' it belonged to Stupin's "Little*

Library" and consisted of such pictures as, for instance, a man carrying a house on his back, a carriage with square wheels, and similar things. This book impressed me very much at that time, because there were many pictures in it about which I could not understand what was absurd in them. They looked exactly like ordinary things in life. And later I began to think that the book really gave pictures of real life, because when I continued to grow I became more and more convinced that all life consisted of "obvious absurdities." Later experiences only strengthened this conviction.' [1]

The difference between today's situation and Ouspensky's is, perhaps, that the absurdities are performed with utter transparency and are neon-lit with bright arrows flashing and pointing down at them. And yet they are accepted at worst and at best treated with mute indifference, unchallenged by significant numbers of the populace. It might be that this is an aspect of what is referred to as the 'post-modern condition' where everything is a simulacrum and a cheap imitation of things that we have stored in our collective imagery about the past, enabling a feeble imitation of institutional structures to continue whilst any content is drained leaving it as a decorative front barely disguising the shoddy casino within. A large part of the public accepts this as a normative state in a world that has become dominated by grift, graft, scam and egregious mendacity. The "*I-know-you-know-I-know-you-know*" smirks of Boris Johnson when being interviewed, in a way, captures our time perfectly: the man much of the mainstream part of the Jewish communities supported who had written a book where 'he portrays a Jewish character, Sammy Katz, with a "proud nose and curly hair", and paints him as a malevolent, stingy, snake-like Jewish businessman who exploits immigrant workers for profit.'[2] The Mad Hatter state of politics meant that this was not a major problem to the mainstream part of the Jewish communities of the UK. Part of the explanation of this, I think, is that in the postmodern world, Johnson hides

---

1   Ouspensky, *In Search of the Miraculous,* Paul H. Crompton, p. 3
2   https://www.theguardian.com/politics/2019/dec/11/boris-johnsons-record-of-bigotry-antisemitism-and-far-right-politics-must-not-be-forgotten

behind the get out clauses of the 'cheeky chappie'[3] whose apparent louche charm permits the traditional drawing room antisemitism associated with his social class. "I was only joking don't ya know" is the implicit background mantra carried by this pseudo-ironic stance, whilst patting 'official' Jews on the head for being good populists and waving a Union Jack amongst the sky blue *Magen Dovid's*. This self-conscious, 'cheeky chappie' role is almost impossible to puncture, hence Johnson's success and arguable popularity within a certain sector of the public. This posture creates its own defences against being gainsaid due to it forcing its own stance on any interlocutor. Everything is posited as a 'laugh' and a 'scam,' so to try and be serious in such a context is to inevitably look silly like some party pooper breaking the *sensus communis* when everyone is having a roaringly good time. It works as a sort of ultimate form of self-empowerment that appears to challenge the establishment whilst simultaneously being it. It's a neat trick but neat tricks are needed when there are fears that the wealth extraction party looks like it might be nearing its end and looking decidedly wobbly. In this manner it was possible for Johnson to be a flagrant antisemite whilst being a philosemite at the same time as, simultaneously, a lifelong anti-racist was portrayed as an antisemite and - a racist!

The smirk of the post-modern politician (think of Johnson's hint of a smile, twinkle in the eye and Michael Gove's raised eyebrows and cameo of the vicar caught *in flagrante delecto*) combined with what can only be described as oral flatulence and flannelling made sense as a form of *post-modern parlance* where everything was a form of mickey-take. Corbyn, perhaps, represented a challenge to this *postmodernist parlance,* his whole manner contrasting with the crass pastiche of politics, reintroducing the 'modernist' notion that there is a narrative, that narrative being the improvability of the world and a reuptake of this stance as an act of returning to real, serious, human concerns. But the postmodern context in which that was delivered did not allow for its survival for very long despite significant support, particularly from young voters. The return to parody

---

3   The appellation 'cheeky chappie' as applied to Johnson has little to do with the type exemplified by Max Miller, who also carried that title. Miller was from a working class background whereas Johnson's class background is more to do with being a faux bumbling and stuttering toff who says 'naughty' things. It's a throw back to P. G. Woodhouse but is now a thoroughly self-conscious, post-modern creation designed for an infantilised public dumbed down by years of 'blingy,' wealth worshipping television and crude and caricatured evolutionary psychology justifications for worshipping wealth and tolerating vast inequality.

politics was very swift. But it wasn't even parody, as Frederick Jameson explains, rather pastiche which eschews the *purposefulness* of parody:

> *'In this situation parody finds itself without a vocation; it has lived, and that strange new thing pastiche slowly comes to take its place. Pastiche is, like parody. The imitation of a peculiar or unique, idiosyncratic style, the wearing of a linguistic mask, speech in a dead language. But it is a neutral practice of such mimicry, without any of parody's ulterior motives, amputated of the satiric impulse, devoid of laughter and of any conviction that alongside the abnormal tongue you have momentarily borrowed, some healthy linguistic normality still exists.'*[4]

Likewise, it was possible for Keir Starmer to get elected then transparently reveal that he had ditched almost all of the pledges[5] he had explicitly signed up to in order to hasten that election, whilst imitating (more pastiche) being a man of 'integrity and sincerity,' as well as mouthing repeatedly that he was combatting antisemitism as he suspended Jews who didn't fit his philosemitic definitions of what constitutes a 'Jew.'[6] In another world, this would have mattered, yet there was no pillorying from the press, no jaw gaping outrage – it was considered a sort of '*as-you-do*,' normative behaviour.

In a number of exchanges I had on Twitter with other Jewish people who had bought the New Antisemitism smears hook line and sinker, there were claims that Johnson, using clichéd antisemitic tropes in his infantile 'novel' had, in reality, only written ' a humorous novel' using a 'literary device where the author distanced himself from the depicted character' to put such antisemitic stereotyping in an implicitly critical light. This, of course, was an utterly desperate gloss given the thundering banality of Johnson's offering. No such techniques of 'distancing' were in play at all, of course, in a crude and trashy novel created as a vulgar and cheap laugh for puerile populist purposes. Yet the use of a caricature Jew, created almost

---

4   Frederick Jameson, *Postmodernism or the Cultural Logic of Late Capitalism*, p. 17
5   https://www.independent.co.uk/news/uk/politics/keir-starmer-labour-conference-pledges-b1928605.html
6   https://www.middleeasteye.net/news/uk-labour-antisemitism-accused-purging-jews-over-claims

no concern and no condemnations from a Chief Rabbi that thought the 'soul of the nation' was at stake. As I type these words, I of course accept the impotence of what I write in the face of the knowing smirk and raised eyebrow, the postmodern gurning that dominates our political discourse based on the 'nudge nudge, wink wink' of the pre-political correctness world of British comedy that was built into the cheap nostalgia that fuelled the diversionary culture war. It seemed that this was the only real constituent of the last and desperate iteration of 'British exceptionalism.' In some ways, Johnson was voicing a sort of truth about our times where everything is a pastiche and not to be taken as referring to anything 'real.' Even the Ukraine war, a tragic development of proportions yet to be unfolded, where Johnson tried to bolster his image with visits to Kiev, largely as a journey man for American interests, was accompanied by buffoonish grins and the ubiquitous thumbs up[7]. As we have observed, as Corbyn was the sudden intervention of a 'serious' stance that pointed to real issues and concerns that harked back to aspects of a modernism that concerned itself with an improvable world, Johnson returns us to a world where everything is cheap imitation with no foundational narrative other than photocopies of sagging imagery from the bloated stockpile of the past.

The *post modern parlance* world of a Johnson avails itself of this empty positioning where lying is transparent and the pastiche such as the Churchillian body language, the large cuffs sticking out of the sleeves. the screwed up eyes and compressed lips mimicking someone taking his interlocutor seriously; the staccato, bumbling mock stutter – all this was hugely popular because it echoed the desire to live in a world of pound-shop pastiche, the mainstay of populism that lives in clichéd images of a putative past. This pastiche and a policy of transparent lying was made abundantly clear in a well known interview from 2006 where he relished stating that "I've got a brilliant new strategy which is to make so many gaffes, that no one knows what to concentrate on." The self-revelatory transparency is also part of the pastiche itself, combined with an abounding sense of massive self-esteem, stentorian vocal confidence and an inbuilt feeling of the invulnerability provided by wealth and social status. This was, to an extent, anticipated by previous politicians

---

7   https://responsiblestatecraft.org/2022/09/02/diplomacy-watch-why-did-the-west-stop-a-peace-deal-in-ukraine/

such as Silvio Berlusconi and the UK's very own Alan Clark and a history of pastiche in politics might well be a subject worthy of a book in itself. Often there is a sort of collusion between the '*piss-take*' and a public that knows it is having the uric acid siphoned out of it but finds this form of locution entertaining, possibly because of decades of being plied with such 'humour.' This seems to disable annoyance and possible anger is neutralised. An American sociologist, researching Trump voters, noted that one interviewee stated that he knew Trump was lying but felt 'seen' by him. Johnson also sensed that he, likewise, had an audience of those ready for this postmodern pastiche. Neo-liberalism itself issued in a period of brazen scam, rip-off, grift, graft and crude cupidity, fragmenting us all into units of self-preservation where becoming a con merchant, including conning ourselves, was psychologically and socially acceptable.

There are many more 'obvious absurdities' we can recount regarding the vast con that was the 'antisemitism crisis.' Aside from the Johnson antisemitism which also included him having employed a vicious antisemite whilst editor of The Spectator – both classic cases of antisemitism which would have been understood as such in the past before the aura of 'pastiche' created an escape tunnel – the Tory Party was, indeed, 'rife' with similar incidents. There were, in no particular order:

The Tory Mayor and the Swastika hot cross bun.[8]

The Tory Councillor with a dubious tattoo with Nazi overtones.[9]

A Tory minister making references to George Soros considered to be reminiscent of 'far-right antisemitic rhetoric.'[10]

The self-same minister using an antisemitic trope connecting two Jewish M.Ps with the 'Illuminati.'[11]

---

8   https://www.portsmouth.co.uk/news/politics/swastika-hot-cross-bun-row-sees-portsmouth-conservative-councillor-lee-mason-suspended-from-tory-party-2539985 After his suspension, the councillor was reinstated three months later   https://www.portsmouth.co.uk/news/politics/swastika-hot-cross-bun-tory-councillor-lee-mason-reinstated-conservative-party-2955122 Swastikas are a 'bit of a laugh' apparently.

9   https://www.dailyrecord.co.uk/news/scottish-news/tory-councillor-hot-water-after-11798420

10   https://www.jewishnews.co.uk/lord-alf-dubs-calls-for-jacob-rees-mogg-to-be-sacked-over-george-soros-comment/

11   Ibid.

Tory Parliamentary candidate suspended for Holocaust denial comment, then reinstated.[12]

Another Tory candidate investigated for alleged antisemitism.[13] Then elected.

Tory student society party where a Hitler moustache is worn as well as shirts carrying the message 'F*ck the NHS.' [14]

Two Tories, one an M.P at the time, the other a councillor and an London Conservative Association Chair pictured dressed in Nazi uniform.[15]

Tory Council candidate deselected after tweeting 'keep the Aryan race going' to a Jewish Labour M.P.[16]

Two Tory council candidates investigated for antisemitism.[17] One is ditched the other is retained after an investigation considered his post 'not-antisemitic.' The Jewish Representative Council for Manchester and Regions states that they consider 'the universally accepted definition on anti-Semitism has been breached' by both candidates, *despite there being no universally accepted definition of antisemitism!*[18]

---

12 https://www.theguardian.com/politics/2019/nov/19/tory-aberdeen-candidate-ryan-houghton-suspended-holocaust-tweets The reinstatement: https://www.thenational.scot/news/18502563.tories-lift-suspension-aberdeen-councillor-anti-semitism-islamophobia-row/ Worth noting that while the Scottish Conservatives condemned antisemitism and Islamophobia they had no problem backing a Party leader who, not withstanding the 'Cheeky Chappie' escape routes, evinced both.

13 https://www.theguardian.com/politics/2019/dec/11/tories-open-second-investigation-sally-ann-hart-hastings-candidate The candidate went on to win the Hastings seat with a majority of over 4,000.

14 https://metro.co.uk/2018/10/03/tory-students-wear-fk-the-nhs-t-shirt-and-hitler-tache-on-uni-night-out-8001669/

15 https://www.google.com/search?q=Tory+dresses+as+Nazi&rlz=1C1CHBF_en-GBGB902GB902&oq=Tory+dresses+as+Nazi&aqs=chrome..69i57.5902j0j15&sourceid=chrome&ie=UTF-8 and https://www.bbc.co.uk/news/uk-england-london-61112219

16 https://www.theguardian.com/news/2021/feb/08/tory-council-candidate-deselected-antisemitic-tweet-to-jewish-labour-mp-charlotte-nichols

17 https://www.manchestereveningnews.co.uk/news/greater-manchester-news/conservatives-ditch-election-candidate-following-23674410

18 They refer to the non-legally binding 'definition' which has been adopted by 37 countries. Far from universal. It is still called a 'working definition' which is, inherently an oxymoron. A feature of the antisemitism weaponisation is to make exaggerated claims about unity in the Jewish communities and unity around the IHRA 'working definition.'

There are more examples that could have been added but the important thing to remember here is that it was the Labour Party that apparently had the crisis, initiated the *Chakraborty Report* and was, eventually, the subject of a stunningly dubious BBC *Panorama* programme and an obviously flawed investigation by a politically skewed entity called the *Equalities and Human Rights Commission* that was considered by many to be unfit for its stated purpose. More obvious absurdities. Antisemitism itself was treated as if it were the object of pastiche and maybe, arguably the type of 'Jew' being presented by the mainstream authorities was also a sort of pastiche. But the obvious thing to note here is that in all the examples above, save the last, there was no content connected with issues of justice for Palestinians or critique of Israeli government policies. The New Antisemitism permitted, it seems, sporting a Hitler moustache, baking a Swastika into a bun, dressing up in Nazi uniform, connecting Jewish M.P's with the Illuminati, Holocaust denial and eulogising the Aryan race without tarnishing the Party to which these actors belonged and moreover, said Party still retaining the mainstream Jewish community vote. Hats for 10/6d anyone?

The *Equalities and Human Rights Commission* 'investigation' into antisemitism in the Labour Party' can also be included in our Mad Hatter's party of upside down meanings. For it was not really an investigation into antisemitism, rather it was an investigation into what was *presumed* to be antisemitism largely based on the aura of crisis based on attribution and association that we discussed earlier. There was no attempt at a decent definition of antisemitism or even any process that could discern fields of meaning and rough boundaries. In fact they barely referred to the flawed IHRA which they used as a reference point whilst noting its controversial nature. The report states that:

> *'In the course of the investigation, the Commission may have regard to the International Holocaust Remembrance Alliance's working definition of antisemitism and associated examples, while recognising it is a non-legally binding definition.'*[19]

---

19   EHRC Report, p. 125. https://www.equalityhumanrights.com/sites/default/files/
investigation-into-antisemitism-in-the-labour-party.pdf

By stating that they 'may have regard' to the IHRA so-called 'definition,' it's not clear what other definition they had 'regard' to. The only reference point was the, by then, five year history of smears, false attributions and vague auras. The latter were prodigiously used as their basis it appears.

That the EHRC never analysed what was fundamentally going on in the Labour Party at that time which was a

> *'bitter struggle between political factions within the Party, and an equally acrimonious conflict both within and outside the Party, over the meaning of antisemitism and its application to the Israel-Palestine dispute,'*

should have, in itself, vitiated the validity of the report.[20] The most important issues germane to an understanding of the nature of the 'crisis' and its manufactured nature were comprehensively ignored in a way that would entitle one to cry out *"you could not make it up."* The fact that the EHRC ignored this most vital and importance evidence – the leaked report that threw light on internal undermining of the leadership - tells us a great deal about the politically skewed nature of the so-called 'investigation.' Jewish campaigner, Andrew Feinstein, who described how he 'watched the Labour antisemitism 'crisis' unfold with a mixture of horror and outrage, as Jeremy Corbyn, a lifelong anti-racist, and the British left in general, have been accused of being antisemitic,'[21] emphasised how this leaked document was central to understanding what was going on behind the scenes in the Labour Party and that

> *'This is crucially important because it shows that whilst the EHRC made selective use of the report, it actively chose not to ask for the underlying evidence on which it was based. If an investigation by a statutory body turns a blind eye to evidence it knows exists, which is vitally relevant to its terms of reference, and which is already collated and organised into an easily accessible format, it simply cannot be considered a full, fair and meaningful investigation.'* [22]

---

20 Geoffrey Bindman QC, in his forward to Jewish Voice for Labour's e-book, *How the EHRC Got It So Wrong*, p. 8.

21 https://truthdefence.org/the-ehrc-report-is-neither-robust-nor-reliable-it-is-deeply-flawed%ef%bf%bc%ef%bf%bc/

22 Ibid.

The report, soon after its release, was hailed as the ultimate 'proof' of 'institutional antisemitism' within the Party despite the fact that determining 'institutional antisemitism' was well outside the frame of reference of the report and something the report certainly did not establish. Despite this the accusation of 'institutional antisemitism' was to be repeated endlessly until it hardened into another unassailable 'truth,' the institutions of the so-called mainstream Jewish community seizing on the EHRC report as the gold standard of truthful representations when that was far from the case. As recently as the last set of council elections, a Labour Council candidate standing in a ward with a significant Jewish community, parroted this falsehood with the confidence of someone who thought their bogus claim was beyond question. Her statement was reported as follows:

> 'A Jewish Labour candidate in Barnet - home to around a quarter of the UK's Jewish population - has apologised to residents for her party being "institutionally anti-Semitic", ahead of next Thursday's all-London council elections. Ella Rose, a Jewish Labour Movement campaigner standing in the Barnet Council elections, told attendees of a London Jewish Forum hustings on Tuesday (April 26) that her party was prejudiced against Jewish people under former leader Jeremy Corbyn - but has now changed.' [23]

And no less than a front bench Labour minister recently did the same. In January 2022, Rachel Reeves stated:

> 'It's very clear what Jeremy Corbyn needs to do. He needs to apologise for his response to the [EHRC] on the Labour Party, which found institutional antisemitism and mistakes made under his leadership.' [24]

---

23   https://www.mylondon.news/news/north-london-news/local-elections-2022-vote-london-23797435 At the time of Ella Rose's utterance, I contacted Barnet Labour Party twice, by e-mail, asking them to explain why Ella Rose was allowed to state such an elemental inaccuracy during the campaign. They did not respond.

24   https://www.thecanary.co/trending/2022/01/21/the-centrists-are-still-twisting-the-truth-about-the-ehrc-report-and-people-arent-having-it/

Reeves went further than this, opining that 'it was a "good thing" Labour membership was dropping as it allowed the party to shed unwelcome supporters and rid itself of the "stain" of anti-Semitism.' The implication being that there were hordes of antisemites amongst those that had left when, as we have noted, figures for 2019 show only 45 individuals were suspended for *alleged* antisemitism using procedures even the deeply flawed and politically skewed EHRC approved, where the bar was set very low for what constituted antisemitism. One needs to roll out the usual old saws here: 'a lie can travel halfway around the world before the truth has got its shoes on' and Nietzsche's 'things are believed that are seen to be believed.' More obvious absurdities. Reeves had form as an apparatchik of the Blairite Right of the Party. In 2013, sensing that the Tory Welfare Reform agenda of stigmatising and vilifying those reliant on welfare, she had opportunistically tried to chime in with the Overton Window on this issue, thinking she could garner future votes by throwing scraps of poor quality meat to the perceived *vox populi*, stating "Labour will be tougher than the Tories on benefits."[25] It was thus no surprise she backed the antisemitism narrative without question.

That the EHRC was politically skewed becomes very clear after only a cursory glance at some of the appointments to the Commission. David Isaacs, appointed as Chair of the EHRC in 2016 was an equity partner in a firm that did legal work for the Government and although he made it clear he would not be involved in such work while holding the post it was still seen as a potential conflict of interest.[26] More directly disturbing in this respect was the case of Pavita Cooper who:

> '[i]n 2013 made a donation of £3,500 to the Conservative party but on her appointment to the commission in 2018 she did not declare any political activity. She and her husband, Steve, held a fundraiser for the then Tory MP for Brentford and Isleworth, Mary Macleod, at which the special guest was George Osborne.'[27]

---

25 https://www.theguardian.com/politics/2013/oct/12/labour-benefits-tories-labour-rachel-reeves-welfare

26 https://www.theguardian.com/society/2020/nov/30/politicising-ehrc-five-controversial-appointments

27 Ibid.

Other appointees were also considered to be politically skewed regarding views on structural racism which clearly could be seen as playing into the populist agenda and the culture war rhetoric of the Tory Party as the last decade progressed. This leaning was further brought out by revelations concerning the ideology of a Board member of the EHRC, one Alisdair Henderson, who actually led the 'inquiry' into 'antisemitism'. He had 'liked' a Tweet whose author opined that:

> 'It's amazing to me that Tory ministers still flounder and flub when some media moron incants the magic words 'misogynist' and 'homophobe', as if those are empirical statements about reality, not highly ideological propaganda terms.'

But perhaps the irony of ironies or, in the context of this chapter's heading, *obvious absurdities of obvious absurdities,* was Henderson's implicit defence of Roger Scruton whose comments on Hungarian Jews put to shame much of the evidence the EHRC itself had adduced as antisemitic. Scrutton had remarked that '[m]any of the Budapest intelligentsia are Jewish, and form part of the extensive networks around the Soros empire.' Henderson's approval of Scruton's right to use such phraseology was expressed in his liking of a Tweet whose author averred that '[i]f Roger Scruton, one of our most esteemed thinkers and writers is drummed out of public life by the offence-taking zealots, we may as well pack up and go home.' That a lead actor in the EHRC Inquiry into Antisemitism in the Labour Party could, at the same time, assent to statements being deemed 'harassment' of a protected category and simultaneously give the green light to an utterance far more unambiguously antisemitic qualifies for a significant *obvious absurdity* award. This raises questions concerning the reliability of someone who can indulge in political leverage of highly *questionable and alleged* antisemitism in one sphere of activity whilst taking a permissive view of indubitable antisemitic viewpoints elsewhere. It is also redolent of hypocrisy and doublespeak that a lead member of the Commision could affirm that words like 'misogynist' and 'homophobe' are 'ideological propaganda terms' while the use of antisemitism as a political and ideological tool is given an air of objectivity.

Shortly before the release of the EHRC Report, the Chair, David Isaacs, resigned referring to the Government wanting someone 'more like their agenda.'[28] It could not be more clear what was going on. In early 2021, Isaacs expanded on his earlier statements without holding back regarding the manner in which the Government was wanting to use the EHRC as part of the culture-war agenda. With reference to the stance of the then Minister for Women and Equalities, he stated:

> *'She says 'I've appointed a new chair and these new commissioners', and she doesn't say 'they're going to do my bidding', but it's pretty implicit in what she's saying that they are people who are supportive of her approach to equalities, which is a focus on white working-class people and the north of England and the levelling up agenda...My view is that an independent regulator shouldn't be in a position where the governments of the day can actually influence the appointments of that body to support a particular ideology.'*

But the job was done and the required damage inflicted. Yet again we, as a society, allowed shoddy, shambolic, poorly evidenced work to become established dogma. As we have observed, this unnervingly parallels the way austerity ideology, the attack on the vulnerable, the grotesquely infantilised Brexit debate and almost every facet of our political life was dumbed-down causing a veritable howling blast of disinformation, comic-book binary simplification and downright manipulative bad faith.

Perhaps a special award of heightened *obvious absurdity* has to go to charges of antisemitism based on the spurious but delightfully Mad Hatterish *'argumentum per pronunciationem'* where Corbyn's authentic, German pronunciation of the name *Epstein* was deemed to be a deliberate accentuation of the latter's Jewish origins. The humour inherent in the American inability to cope with the German *'ei'* which presumably, must have started with the large scale immigration of Jews to the United States in the late 19th and early 20th Centuries, had already been explored in the Mel Brooks film Young Frankenstein where the legendary doctor bemoans the authentic pronunciation of his name, insisting on *'steen.'*[29] Was Mary

28 https://www.theguardian.com/society/2020/aug/08/david-isaac-equalities-chief-bids-farewell-after-four-momentous-years
29 *https://www.youtube.com/watch?v=nxxSIX3fmmo*

Shelley antisemitic in her choice of the name 'Frankenstein?' The levels of absurdity reached would not preclude such an idea.

The farcical furore over this at least had the 'merit' of throwing an eponymous journalist called Angela Epstein into the limelight for five minutes who proclaimed in the esteemed pages of the *Daily Mail*, with carefully manufactured and manicured high dudgeon, how affronted she was that someone should pronounce her name authentically and that it was, without a shred of doubt, a deliberate, antisemitic caricature and that *'Every Jewish person would be offended by the pronunciation.'* [30] She was clearly so horrified and offended that she managed to hide the emotional pain just enough to provide a carefully prepared picture of herself in a self-publicity styled quasi-fashion shot, out of which she seems to be beaming quite contentedly.

The appeal to a mythical, homogenous Jewish reaction, *every Jewish person would…*, as if there were an archetypal Jew conveniently hovering in the ether, is, as we have noted before, typical of the framing of the New Antisemitism and its scattergun accusations. This arrogation to oneself as arbiter of *'the right thinking Jew'* is a form of totalitarian thinking that seeks to marginalise dissent and de-Judaize those within the Jewish communities that differ. The *'every Jewish person would'* is a vocalised equivalent of the political use of phrases like 'the right thinking person,' or, as was noted in the introduction, David Cameron's 'those that do the right thing.' The othering, disenfranchising, marginalising and ostracising is, in effect, more proto-fascistic populism. Angela Epstein clearly milked her five minutes of fame for what it was worth but the vacuity and banality of it all was off the scale.

In his book, *The Identity Myth*, David Swift suggests that Corbyn's authentic German pronunciation of the *'stein'* part of a Jewish name was more connected with a 'woke' attempt to curry favour with Jews which was badly misjudged by Corbyn, who put on

> *'a hammy Yiddish inflection so that Harvey Winestein became Harvey Vine-shtein, and Jeffrey Epstein became Jeffrey Ep-shtein. Many people held this up as an indication of antisemitism, although, personally I*

30   https://www.dailymail.co.uk/debate/article-7708351/Journalist-ANGELA-EPSTEIN-blasts-Jeremy-Corbyns-pronunciation.html

thought it was tin-eared rather than sinister: he was actually trying to endear himself to Jews by showing his learning and cultural sensitivity, too stupid to see it would have the exact opposite effect.[31]

I suspect that Swift was so focussed on trashing Corbyn for his alleged 'political correctness' and strengthening an aspect of his central thesis that a 'woke' Left (and 'anti-woke' Right) were letting down the working class, that he tried to overdrive the point, drawing analogies between this and the way middle class lecturers and football commentators over pronounce names from other countries and cultures as a way of exhibiting a sort of contentless progressiveness. His book makes some very valid observations about the manipulation of identity issues but the idea that Corbyn was using a 'hammy, Yiddish accent' seems utterly bizarre as the names were simply pronounced in a standard German way without any *Fiddler-on-the Roofisms* thrown in. And the notion that Corbyn could be so out of touch as to imagine that returning German-Jewish names back to their original pronunciation would curry favour is a hypothesis too far. In any case, while there may be examples of middle-class neo-colonialists bending over backwards to over accurately pronounce names of those from former colonies with an orientalist condescension, this has never been applied to Jews, nor is there any tradition of it. Thus it appears very unlikely to have been a motivation for Corbyn unless he was inventing a new category of linguistic philosemitism on the spot. More likely is that Corbyn, who speaks fluent Spanish and might have known a bit of German simply chose to pronounce the names authentically.

If the gold medal of obvious absurdities goes to the *'Epshtinerama'* episode a photo-finish contender must surely be Angela Rayner's comments on the suspension of Jeremy Corbyn for pointing out, after the release of the EHRC report, that the scale of antisemitism in the party was very small and leveraged for political purposes. Rayner actually stated, in an interview that she believed

'the statement around the small numbers and to suggest that it is a small number in the Labour Party, whilst

---

31   David Swift, *The Identity Myth*, p. 82

that might be true, is completely unacceptable to not understand the hurt and the distress...' [32]

So Rayner was, apparently, saying that although Corbyn's statement that the scale of the antisemitism *'problem was also dramatically overstated for political reasons by our opponents inside and outside the party'*, might be true, he still shouldn't have said it because a myth has to be sustained in order to not offend that sector of the Jewish communities that needed it to be maintained! Quite incredible and utterly bizarre, so much so that it even negated the EHRC Report's affirmation of Article 10 of the Human Rights Act that backs up Corbyn's right to say what he did. It seems clear that Rayner was getting caught on the barbed wire of her own contradictory position which was the result of playing the apparatchik line for career purposes whilst inadvertently revealing her inner tension by being unable to deny the truism inherent in Corbyn's view.

In a further statement, Rayner, kowtowed much more obsequiously to the antisemitism crisis myth by classically plying the requisite fabrication of homogeneity of a 'Jewish Community':

> *'I'm just deeply, deeply upset by the circumstances and really upset that Jeremy wasn't able to see today the pain that the Jewish community has gone through.'* [33]

What about the pain of those Jews who had been grimacing for years as they witnessed the abuse of the meaning of the tragedy of antisemitism and its relegation to an object of cheap political leverage? They didn't exist, they were rendered invisible whilst a manufactured notion of a united community of one voice was kept afloat and anyone outside this mainstream notion of acceptability was de-Judaized. Rayner's cloying and repulsive performance as a reinvented apparatchik figure of the new Party shaped by Starmer, a person who arguably got elected through a skein of pathological lying and who also, arguably, broke his own Party rules[34] and

---

32 https://skwawkbox.org/2020/10/31/video-rayner-admits-what-corbyn-said-was-true-but-it-was-unacceptable/

33 https://labourlist.org/2020/10/angela-rayner-says-corbyn-has-absolute-blind-spot-on-antisemitism/

34 https://skwawkbox.org/2020/11/19/starmers-suspension-of-corbyn-broke-parliamentary-party-rules-all-of-them/

EHRC injunctions[35] when suspending Corbyn, was yet another sign of this world of inverted realities and what I earlier referred to as *postmodern-piss-take-parlance,* intentionally raising the usually vulgar term '*piss-take*' to that of a term of art. What might have demolished careers in the past was now a *sine qua non* of advancing them. One wonders whether this shock free standing an underlying reality on its head in such a blatant fashion is yet another expression of the postmodern era. Or are we now *post-postmodern* and a term has yet to be invented for it? Perhaps Simon Maginn's reference to a 'post-fraud, post-civility world' hits the mark.[36] Nevertheless, it still seems to fit within postmodernism's breaking down of the sense of continuity and sustainable consistency, in particular a

> *[p]reoccupation with the fragmentation and instability of language...a breakdown in the signifying chain of meaning that creates a simple sentence. When the signifying chain snaps, then 'we have schizophrenia in the form of a rubble of distinct and unrelated signifiers.'... The effect of such a breakdown in the signifying chain is to reduce experience to a 'series of pure and unrelated presents in time.'[37]*

The public are presented with isolated sound bites, politicians continually contradicting themselves, inventing new and ephemeral narratives on an almost daily basis and the whole thing rushes past at such speed that there is no possibility of identifying an underlying 'truth' against which it can be measured. As we observed earlier, Boris Johnson

---

35 https://novaramedia.com/2021/07/27/heres-what-really-happened-when-starmer-suspended-corbyn/ '*The EHRC report had explicitly stated that Labour members were entitled to "express their opinions on internal party matters, such as the scale of antisemitism within the party" – so expelling Corbyn for claiming that the scale had been "overstated" would be difficult. In addition, one of the report's key recommendations was that the disciplinary process over alleged antisemitism should be free from "political interference". It asserted that if "staff from the leader of the opposition's office (LOTO) were able to influence decisions on complaints, especially decisions on whether to suspend someone", this would amount to "unlawful indirect discrimination". So by suspending Corbyn and his allies, Starmer had himself violated the injunctions of the EHRC.'* But of course, very few in the media and in politics cared; a particular aim was achieved.

36 https://simonmaginn.medium.com/on-incivility-and-wellbeing-and-bear-hunts-27c96b4da0a

37 David Harvey: *The Condition of Postmodernity,* p. 53.

was explicit about this and was well aware of how to use this feature of our cultural condition. In this respect, he was significantly less dangerous and disturbing than someone like Kier Starmer who pretends to embody old-fashioned integrity. Ironically, Johnson is arguably the most honest of recent political figures in this respect, an observation that itself seems quite strange and contrarian. What horrified the establishment so much was that Corbyn, by and large, cut across this and suddenly injected a coherent narrative that sustained itself as long as it could before the avalanche of disinformation and collapsed meanings became too much. Corbyn appeared to be a shocking re-entry of modernism into a thoroughly post-modern culture creating an instantaneous *tableau de consternation* amongst the career-threatened media and political class who were surfing with ease a world where nothing really mattered as long as their careers sustained and wealth accrued. The countercultural event was, initially, treated as a joke then taken seriously, very seriously indeed. What Corbyn reintroduced was the old world of modernism that was

> *'about the pursuit of better futures...[b]ut postmodernism typically strips away that possibility by concentrating upon the schizophrenic circumstances induced by fragmentation and all those instabilities (including those of language) that prevent us even picturing coherently, let alone devising strategies to produce, some radically different future.'* [38]

This freedom to say anything and get away with it as long as one said it with blustering conviction and chest inflated confidence, surely reached its apogee with the grotesque and ghastly, phantasmagoric utterance of Simon Heffer that Corbyn 'wants to open the gates of Auschwitz.' This hysterical and hyperbolic leveraging of the calamity of the Holocaust was proportionate to the panic the establishment was feeling that 2017 might repeat itself but this time take Labour just over the winning line. This hideously desperate and plangently absurd overreach of the trajectory of vilification was the last gasp of the inane crescendo of the mad-hattered trouncing of meaning, scale and value that had become normative. In the interview, Heffer added a crowbar of infinite length to his previous leveraging by adding, after being challenged on the acceptability of what

---

38   Ibid. P. 53-54.

he said, that "I'm sure, in 1933, they had similar conversations in Germany: "the Fuehrer's never going to do that."

Heffer's Mad Hatter hat was so firmly rammed onto his head that it must have caused serious pressure on the cranium leading to hallucinogenic excess. But as we have noted, hallucinatory excess is very much a part of this discourse. It was seen as an almost acceptable statement and a useful addition to the armoury of the New Antisemitism arsenal that it received no noticeable kickback from the mainstream part of the Jewish communities despite the disgust many Jews on the left felt at this quasi-pornographic display of Holocaust exploitation. Despite the lack of significant pushback to this from the 'official' bodies, well-known Jews on the Left made it clear what was going on here:

> 'The way charges of anti-Semitism are being used in Britain to undermine the Corbyn-led Labour Party is not only a disgrace, but also – to put it simply – an insult to the memory of the victims of the Holocaust...'. [39]

Gideon Levy, the Israeli journalist, also made it abundantly clear what was going on regarding the link between the U.K Jewish mainstream and the geo-political dimension:

> 'The Jewish establishment in Britain and the Israeli propaganda machine have taken out a contract on the leader of the British Labour Party, Jeremy Corbyn. The contract was taken out a long time ago, and it was clear that the closer Corbyn came to being elected prime minister, the harsher the conflict would get.' [40]

In the not too distant past, Heffer's remarks would have been career ending. They were a sort of mirror image of *Holocaust denial*, a form of what might be called *Holocaust abuse*. But in the world we have identified as *postmodern pastiche,* where even the most horrific images from the past are fair game for exploitation, even this excess appeared acceptable. We have clearly reached the point where, as Enzo Traverso puts it, the Holocaust has becomes a piece of 'embalmed history'[41] and a type of 'civil religion' that can be appealed to in ways that disrespect its elemental

---

39 https://www.scoop.co.nz/stories/WO1912/S00016/reopening-auschwitz-the-conspiracy-to-stop-corbyn.htm

40 Ibid.

41 Enzo Traverso, *The End of Jewish Modernity*, p. 116.

nature so that the shell that is left can be used as a flag or talisman of some sort. The Holocaust itself was thus fair game in ramping up the trashing of Corbyn as the election approached.

At around the same time and not coincidently, so one suspects, a *BBC Panorama* programme, a BBC institution in itself that for many years was portrayed as the ultimate model of objective reporting, produced a supposed 'investigation' into antisemitism in the Labour Party. It largely interviewed those in the Party that had a negative animus towards Corbyn and the leaderships office. In one particular interview which was portrayed as an example of indisputable antisemitism towards a Jewish member of the Party staff, an investigation by *The Canary*,[42] shortly after showed that the alleged 'antisemitic exchange' had not take place and was an interpolation by the staffer to make it appear antisemitic. *The Canary*, an alternative media outlet, was comprehensively ignored, the damning story only re-emerging when an Al Jazeera documentary called *Labour Files*[43] included it as part of a whole series of revelations showing how senior Labour Party staff created a culture of lies and disinformation aimed at discrediting the leadership of their Party. This, in turn, was largely ignored. The almost total ignoring of these revelations was part of the *obvious absurdities* world we are inhabiting. Of course, it was vital that these appalling facts were ignored in order to maintain the unassailability of a myth. Yet again we should be shocked we're not shocked. Perhaps the postmodernist culture of 'continuous present' has rendered us almost impervious to barefaced lies and cavalier and contradictory stances that come at us so thick and fast there is no time to absorb the overwhelming discontinuities and form a coherent picture, this combined with a largely stressed, time poor populace is the perfect recipe for numb indifference.

---

42   https://www.thecanary.co/investigations/2019/07/19/fresh-testimony-from-labour-members-could-blow-panoramas-antisemitism-claims-wide-open/ The title of the article was *'Fresh testimony from Labour members could blow Panorama's antisemitism claims wide open'* was ignored at the time, resurfacing in an Al Jazeera documentary in December 2022 and ignored again, the BBC programme, by now resting cosily in the armchair of 'established truth' that propped up the bogus narrative. Starmer's refusal to challenge John Ware, the producer of the Panorama programme, who had brought a libel case against the Party and who simply paid off Ware and the so-called whistleblowers was, in effect, an expression of Starmer's desire to prop up a false narrative. The case was deemed winnable according to legal advice the Party had received.

43   https://twitter.com/caitoz/status/1574335646528724992

Many more pages could be filled with these *obvious absurdities* but as the length of this chapter, in the context of the scope of this book, has to be of reasonably limited proportions I'll end on one last one that pertains to this book's parodying title. The idea that *'Jews don't count'* has been rendered even more patently absurd by the concerns raised around *hierarchies of racism* which was a result of the political leverage of antisemitism to an obsessive degree at the expense of other minorities. Given the racism apparent in the language of senior Labour staffers in the 860 page leaked report[44] and Starmer's paying off the producer of those involved in the misleading and dis-informative *Panorama* programme,

> *'members of the BAME staff network warned that the apologies to seven ex-staffers who appeared on BBC Panorama could further a perception of a "hierarchy of racism" in the party, with antisemitism seen as the most serious form of prejudice, while Islamophobia and anti-black racism were considered less important.'* [45]

The only inaccuracy in the above is the implication that antisemitim was being taken seriously as a prejudice. It was only apparently being taken seriously whilst it was being weaponised and the meaning abused. Real antisemitism was not being taken seriously at all as we have seen in relation to the Tory Party. Nevertheless, the focus on even a largely leveraged form of antisemitism was, as the passage states, to the detriment of the other issues mentioned. The recent release of the *Forde Report* whilst undermining the assertions of the EHRC Report and the Panorama programme strengthened the contention even further that there was a hierarchy of racism in the Labour Party due to the leveraging of alleged antisemitism to a behemothic degree. The black M.P., Kate Osamor spelled this out:

> *'It's worth remembering what it is that the leadership is dismissing. Forde found problems of discrimination in the party. In particular, he cited concerns by party members over a perceived "hierarchy of racism" leading*

---

44 https://novaramedia.com/2022/07/29/it-was-just-relentless-black-and-muslim-labour-councillors-reveal-experiences-of-party-racism/

45 https://www.theguardian.com/politics/2020/aug/13/hierarchy-of-racism-fears-threaten-starmers-hopes-of-labour-unity

to "many other forms of racism and discrimination" being overlooked due to a focus on allegations of antisemitism.' [46]

Osamor, in her Open Democracy article, emphasises how Starmer tried to downplay the at times radical implications of the *Forde Report* in order to prop up the false narrative that this was all connected with the Corbyn era and not the factionalism that he himself was part of:

> The Labour leader said he "didn't need the report to tell me we needed to take action". Starmer also claimed the report, which he commissioned and which collected evidence from the party while he was leader, was merely a historical document that reflected the party under its previous stewardship. [47]

Of course, Starmer had to downplay the *Forde Report* from an existential point of view, for to have brought out the implications of it would have meant the shipwreck of significant parts of the 'antisemitism crisis' narrative and put a spotlight on the undemocratic undermining of the Party leadership by its own officers during the Corbyn years. Starmer was ably assisted in this downplay by the mainstream media, as *Novara Media* put it:

> As soon as the report was out, Labour party spinners reached out to favourable journalists. Rather than read the report, and inform their audiences of its contents, several simply repeated the spokesperson's words verbatim –with the i-Newspaper's Paul Waugh even doing so without quotation marks. To the ordinary person, Labour's claim that the report "completely debunks the conspiracy theory that the 2017 general election was somehow deliberately sabotaged" comes across as Waugh's own conclusion, rather than the words of a party press officer.

---

46   https://www.opendemocracy.net/en/keir-starmer-forde-report-racism-labour-kate-osamor-mp/

47   Ibid.

This is 'churnalism', where journalists simply repeat the lines of press teams and releases without doing actual work or reporting themselves. It's one rung below fake news on the ladder of journalistic ethics. For the public, such a lack of professionalism can make it hard to know what to believe, the truth secondary to an information war peddled by certain factional interests who are aided by friendly journalists and pundits.[48]

As I type these words, I note that the Labour Party Conference has just ended. It was held during the Jewish New year (*Rosh HaShannah*) a fact that should have rendered it offensive to mainstream Jews but miraculously didn't. There was no noisy outcry. A prominent Jewish member of the National Executive council was peremptorily suspended[49] just before Conference began. Jews are at least five times as likely to be suspended and investigated by the Labour Party, a fact that also caused no outcry in the mainstream community. During Conference, the Party bragged about 'dealing with antisemitism'; a delegate is suspended who speaks out against the policy of NATO and the EU in relation to Ukraine;[50] there is a great show of apparent 'unity' and the mainstream media heralds Starmer as ready to be the next Prime Minister. Top hats are on sale in the foyer in the pre-decimal currency of ten shillings and sixpence.

---

48 https://novaramedia.com/2022/07/19/the-forde-report-proves-the-labour-machine-was-rotten-to-its-core/

49 https://labourlist.org/2022/09/labour-nec-member-suspended-for-speaking-at-proscribed-groups-event/

50 https://morningstaronline.co.uk/article/b/labour-conference-delegate-suspended-after-opposing-arming-ukraine

Chapter 6

"If You're an Antisemite, I'm a Jew" [1]

The title of this chapter was the response of Erik H. Erikson, the great pioneer of developmental psychology, to one of his teachings assistants, who, perplexed by the presence of a crucifix in Erikson's room, asked him if he now identified as a Christian or as a Jew. Thinking about this intriguing response from a very self-aware psychologist, I realised it could be interpreted in two ways: as a statement which shows how an external force, in the form of antisemitism, can define someone as a Jew regardless of how they see themselves. This latter is a negative form of identity where Erikson is saying: "if you are antisemitic, you will see me as a Jew." The second interpretation is much more positive and could be read as the assumption of a Jewish identity *because* of antisemitism. Here, Erikson would be saying: "I'm going to positively identify as a Jew in order to challenge your antisemitism in the spirit of challenging a specific, irrational prejudice. In this spirit I could adopt other identities should your prejudice have taken a different focus." For an orthodox Jew such as the former Chief Rabbi, Immanuel Jakobovits, both ways of identifying as a Jew would have been classed as a negative form of identification: reluctant identity by dint of antisemitism or identification as an act of combatting prejudice. In a discussion on the identity dilemmas surrounding issues of Jews as a religion and Jewishness as a nationality that the existence of Israel stirred up which will be discussed later in this chapter, Jakobovits was firmly of the view that strict Jewish, rabbinical law must be the determining factor. In 1971, after he made his views public by writing to then Israeli Prime Minister on this issue, he received this response from Leo Abse, a Labour Member of Parliament:

---

1   See: *Identity's Architect, A biography of Erik H. Erikson*, p. 315.

The Chief Rabbi of a section of British Jewry, with extraordinary presumption, has sought to interfere with the ruling of the supreme court of a sovereign state. He is reported to have cabled the Prime Minister of Israel asking her to reverse the ruling of the Israeli Supreme Court that the children of a non-religious Jew and a Scotswoman may, at the choice of the parents, be registered as Jews...As Ben Gurion has remarked, a Jew is someone who calls himself one; and I shall call myself one as long-to quote another secular Jew Ilya Ehrenburg-as there is antisemitism.[2]

This literary encounter on the issue of 'who is a Jew' goes to the heart of much of the debate that is still current. But for Erikson, the psychologist who wrote so much about identity and for whom a Jewish identity was never an unambiguous given, his own, personal response is highly significant and throws light on the nature of identity itself and its psychological and social roots. In more recent years, the notion of 'who is a Jew' and Jewish identity in general has been the subject of much debate and this in itself raises questions about how identity is assumed, its role in discourses of power, access to resources and its manipulation for geo-political purposes. These issues figured strongly, as we have seen, in the so-called 'antisemitism crisis' in the Labour Party which created a 'good,' mainstream and politically powerful Jew against the 'bad,' left wing, or sometimes orthodox Jew who didn't sustain the official narrative around the use of antisemitism. The latter were usually rendered 'beyond the pale' (to use an historically loaded term) and largely deprived of a voice. For example, the journalist Jonathon Freedland's so-called play *'Jews in Thier Own Words'* produced at The Royal Court Theatre, largely props up the 'official' narrative of an antisemitism crisis on the Left with no room for the significant alternative Jewish voices that challenge this. 'Jews' here, simply meaning 'officially sanctioned, approved Jews.'[3] The illusion of the monolith, once more, as Naomi Idrissi Wimbourne puts it:

---

2   I. Jakobovits: *If Only My People...Zionism in My Life*, pp. 195-196

3   https://www.jewishvoiceforlabour.org.uk/article/review-of-freedlands-jews-in-their-own-words-by-naomi-wimborne-idrissi/

Freedland's play epitomises the hot mess we have been living through since the end of 2015 – a period when the word "antisemitism" has been bandied about almost endlessly without the reality it represents being honestly elucidated. Those who tried to examine contending definitions of antisemitism – such as ourselves and academic experts in the field like Antony Lerman, Brian Klug and David Feldman – were almost entirely blanked by mainstream media, or drowned out by Freedland and friends. How about a play giving voice to those who have genuinely been silenced? That could make for interesting theatre![4]

Freedland, then, presents an ossified view of Jewish identity which presupposes a Zionist bent alongside what is arguably a politically distorted view of what constitutes antisemitism. As Idrissi points out, an opportunity was lost to create something more illuminating and genuinely explorative rather than a one dimensional presentation shorn of the real complexity behind it. In short, it was another form of manufacturing consent. Jews were being pressured into seeing themselves in a particular way. When dissent is suppressed, either explicitly or implicitly, the latter form being the more insidious because of its easy deniability, we end up with a form of totalitarianism, a point which according to media lens and distinguished journalist Peter Oborne, we have almost reached.[5]

Identity, operates on different levels and at its most basic and fundamental level, as explored by Erikson, is thought to be about forming a cohesive sense of feeling like a person who sustains through time and does not fragment and collapse and

'consists of bodily constitution and command thereof, mental capacities, family and wider social relations, and cultural heritage all wound into one cohesive thread that persists through time without major breaks.'[6]

---

4   Ibid.
5   https://twitter.com/OborneTweets/status/1578105961696604160
6   Florian Coulmas, *Identity, A Very Short Introduction,* p. 93.

Sometimes, this appears to go 'wrong' and names are given to quasi medically defined conditions for this such as 'borderline personality disorder' and other supposed pathologies where a sense of the boundaries between self and not-self become very porous to the degree where daily functioning is impaired. We might consider these issues connected with a very basic sense of 'ego-identity,' a minimum level of which can be considered a sine qua non for maintaining a life.

There is also another level of identity connecting with identifying with 'things' and 'images of the self.' As we live in a culture where mental health is considered to be 'epidemic,' questions are raised around the nature of 'self' and the need to psychologically identify with being something in particular. Just as there is a pressure to 'have' things so there is a pressure to 'have' the mental furniture of being somebody and identifying as someone. These are, of course, questions embedded in the particular culture that has thrown them up. It is this latter that is of interest in relation to the antisemitism issue and what it means to identify as a Jew, for to even consider oneself as a Jew or be considered a Jew is, for many in this existential situation, to question the function of the psychology of identity itself, as one Jewish writer, in considering herself to be a Jew, conveys so well:

> 'For me (as for all Jews, I believe), Jewishness isn't a comfortable background against which I can play out other complex dramas of subjectivity and identity. Because I have to construct my own Jewishness in the world and continue to have to do so, I also have to deconstruct my Jewishness. The kind of Jew I am is the kind who isn't sure what kind of Jew I am.'[7]

The above passage portrays the state of awareness of being Jewish as an existential dilemma, as a real challenge to psychological security, as an enjoinder to work through, inquire about and research that which can so easily and glibly be taken for granted. We now live in a period of time where identity is fetishistically exploited like a commodity, where hanging your hat on the hatstand of national, ethnic and postural identities has become a market place in itself. Witness the Remain/Brexit divide which was used as a great decoy mechanism, diverting people away from the much

---

7   Maria Damon, *Word-Landslayt, in People of the Book*, p. 386.

more trenchant economic and environmental issues that were materially affecting their lives. A battle ensued between those identifying as 'liberal cosmopolitans' against doughty nationalists putting the 'Great back into Britain' whilst housing remained unaffordable, wages low, private debt high and social services crumbling. Yet it was identity that fuelled the polarised cultural scenario with each side driven by the need to preserve their respective psychological security in their perceived rectitude. Each side seemed to white knuckle their self-image as if the very coherence of their psyches depended on it. Clearly identity is a powerful driving force where

> *'issues around 'identity' allow extremists and bad faith actors – on both Left and Right – to rise to prominence, power and financial success on the backs of people they don't really understand and often despise. In many cases these identities have become powerful signifiers in their own right, detached from any material realities and instrumentalised, idealised and imitated. Their boundaries are policed and their significance exploited, so that the identities themselves matter more than the lives of the individuals concerned.'* [8]

Given the ease with which identity can be manipulated to create a 'feel good factor' should we not welcome the psychological discomfort that questioning the flaccid acceptance of identity creates? If this questioning arises that more acutely as a result of considering one's Jewishness then it is worth exploring whether that aspect of Jewishness might not be one of its most valuable components, a component that has significantly given way to a 'new' concept of Jewishness that, linked to Zionism and ethno-nationalism, has become another easily donned identity and fervid flag wave. Identity, in the sense we are now talking about, can serve a purpose of providing a spurious psychological security based on a continuous need to affirm a certain image of the self. This attempt to shore up this 'security' via the mental stabilisers of identity has been challenged by the more esoteric aspects of differing religious traditions and figures connected with related spiritual and psychological insights. Krishnamurti put it like this:

---

8   David Swift, *The Identity Myth*, p. ix.

So this central issue is whether one can exist healthily, sanely, harmoniously without identifying with anything, not only outwardly but inwardly - identifying myself with my experience, identifying oneself with the family, with beliefs, with institutions and so on. That means can one live in this world with no identification? Which means can one live harmoniously, both with the outer and the inner without any sense of occupation and identification? Is this clear? Let's be clear of the problem first before we operate on it. When one is occupied with oneself, with one's body, with one's beauty, with one's eyes - you know, this constant occupation with oneself, you deny actually all relationship, though you may sleep with another, though you may hold hands with another, say 'What a darling you are' - all the rest of it, but the identification process separates human beings. And from that, violence, wars, division of races, everything takes place. Right?

Now the next question is: whether it is possible to live in this world daily without any sense of identification? Not only with the senses - the body - but with the name, with all the past, the heredity - you understand? - the Englishman, the German, all the history of all the past, to be completely free from all that and yet live in harmony with activity in daily life. Is this problem clear now? [9]

Krishnamurti asks this question not as a statement concerning whether we can or should live without identification but puts it as a process of inquiry which must be constantly renewed in order to be alert to the activity of thought which creates that identification. Even seeing oneself as a liberal universalist can be yet another self-image though it may appear to be a 'good' or 'preferable' one which results in another power structure that identification creates. Jews as outsiders have often implicitly raised discomfiting issues around identity and perhaps this implicit questioning of the ostensible firmness of identification has been an element in the animosity directed towards them at certain junctures in the history of the countries in which they were present where

---

9   https://jkrishnamurti.org/content/identification-thought

*'the difference of the outsider can illuminate problems
and ambiguites, raise questions about issues that have
been take for granted, criticize the received notions, or
even suggest alternative modes of behaving/or thinking.
That is why the Nazi hates the Jew.'* [10]

But now we have the 'Jew as insider', the 'new Jew' as sociologist
Shlomo Sand put it.[11] Jewish identity has, particularly in the post-Six
Day War, world become a strong, secular image as well as a religious
one. When I was briefly at a religious seminary (*Yeshiva*) in Jerusalem as
a young man, some of the Rabbis directing the institution very sensibly
expressed concern that recent arrivals from secular backgrounds, eager
to don a new-found religious identity fuelled by their excessive zeal,
would suddenly grow 'ringlets' (*Peyot*) as if they were fashion accessories.
The Rabbis wisely discouraged this sensing that it was a pure image and
certainly not applicable to a religion that eschewed the 'graven image'
which might be considered a sort of cognate of the images that surround
our modern sense of identity. However, modern Israel has furnished us
with the 'Settler,' 'distinguished by a set of symbolic identifiers: knitted
skull cap, Biblical sandals, *tzitzit* and automatic rifle and beard.'[12] Hanging
your hat on this latter form of identification clearly has significant,
real world consequences yet might have its roots in the same forms of
identification that appear to be less immediately harmful and divisive. In
other words, it is the product of the same psychological drives.

We now live in an age dominated not only by tidal waves of images but
by the history of images themselves. Over a hundred years of advertising
images used with a consciously manipulative technique derived from the
insights of psychology and psychoanalysis became part of an intensified
consumption culture that continuously expanded its scope right up to the
contemporary bombardment of social media. Identity, in the modern sense,
arrives on waves of images which become internalised and marketable.
Has identity, including modern Jewish identity, become a mere image
in the market place of images that have been manufactured to prop up
psyches that would otherwise flounder given a culture so saturated with

---

10   Raphael Sassower, The "Jew" as "Postmodern": A Personal Report, in The People of the Book, p. 302.

11   See: Shlomo Sand, *How I Stopped Being a Jew*, p. 91

12   Gilad Atzmon, The Wandering Who, p. 46.

forms of identification? The conflation of Zionism with Jewishness, is itself another creation of an image of the 'new Jew' and a type of 'fictional creation of ethnic unity'[13] which relies on 'the image of soldiers of the IDF, svelte and spirited, perched on powerful armoured cars or leaning proudly against jet fighters.' The image 'serves as an identity card for many Jews throughout the world.'[14] Many Jewish people see this as a welcome development representing strength and power after centuries of perceived weakness, excessive humility and psychological vacillation about who one was.

The lower of the two images on the front of this book shows this '*new Jew*' identity in confident and ebullient action in the UK, the Israeli flags and the embedded toadyism of the single Union Jack demonstrating fealty to the integration of British populism with the related ethno-nationalism of the post '67 Jewish identity. The image reeks of power, certainty and a vulgar display of surly indentarian values. It is no surprise that, in recent decades, the right wing, despite being traditionally antisemitic and who still express antisemitic views, have been comfortable appropriating Zionism to their populist cause. As far back as 1978, a researcher into British neo-Nazi National Front movement found a strange ability of some of its members to hold antisemitic and anti-Zionist attitudes whilst praising Israel for the way it stands up for itself, no doubt a quality they wanted Britain to manifest in a more aggressive manner:

> *The interviewees who believed in the [Jewish] conspiracy theory used the concept of 'Zionism' almost exclusively in its conspiracy tradition sense...The word was seldom used in its customary mainstream sense of the movement designed to create and now maintain the Jewish State of Israel. When Israel was mentioned, it was done so perfunctorily...The abstraction of the concept of 'Zionism' from the reality of Israel into the half-digested conspiracy mythology of the interviewees produced some bizarre statements. K[an interviewee]...expressed himself as being anti-Zionist [in the 'Jewish conspiracy' sense]...also expressed praise for Israel: 'I've got a lot*

---

13   Shlomo Sand, *How I Stopped Being a Jew*, p. 49.
14   Ibid. p. 93-94.

of sympathy for the Israeli people. I do feel strongly for them. I think they are a great nation. I really do... and whatever they've wanted they've stood up and fought for.' [15]

This quote is, perhaps, an early example and anticipation of how the Right would become more pro- Israel as time went on. In recent years, with the culture wars and its attendant Islamophobia this support has become much more demonstrative with ex- *English Defence League leader* Tommy Robinson parading himself on an Israeli tank and embarrassingly for the Board of Deputies, turning up at a pro-Israel rally in London. Other right wing groups in the UK such as Britain First have also linked up with pro-Israeli movements. It is now clear that these groups have, indeed, become strange bedfellows. This is also mirrored by the Evangelical Right in America where open or latent antisemitism is not a disqualifier for supporting Israel politically.

One of the most powerful, iconic images behind this contemporary, hot-housed, form of Jewish identity must surely be that of the beatific face of the Israeli paratrooper taking part in the 'liberation' of the 'Wailing Wall,' his helmet removed, giving the impression of an almost Christian, *Angelus* gesture, his emotions tangible.[16] This is an image I grew up with which in a strange way became a sort of burden, enjoining one, as it does, to feel a sense of awe and devotion around that sacred symbol. As someone who has never experienced military combat and its emotional impact, it felt impertinent to even question what a soldier like this had fought for. He was fighting for 'us' wasn't he? And certainly the horrors of war suffered by anyone should be respected as a reality completely out of the grasp of those who have been lucky enough not to have experienced them. When I briefly lived in Jerusalem, I found little sense of connection with those stones which were, by then, part of a neatly paved piazza and seemed to me to be a sort of film set, a fetishised image that was designed to trigger a sense of identity. Far removed from the narrow passage way it originally was, back then it was fronted by ad hoc structures which had been erected in the area and was known as the *Mughrabi Quarter.* This area of dwellings was destroyed within days of the end of the so-called Six Day War leaving

---

15   Michael Billig: Fascists. *A Social Psychological View of the National Front.* p. 305. Quoted and edited in: W.D. Rubenstein: *The Left, the Right and the Jews,* p. 81.

16   https://en.wikipedia.org/wiki/Paratroopers_at_the_Western_Wall

many refugees. Perhaps it was because the Wall was to immediately become a fetishised and commoditised symbol that Yeshiyahu Leibowitz referred to the Western Wall as the *Discotel* (a portmanteau word and a play on "discothèque" and "Kotel", the latter a transliterated Hebrew word which literally means "wall", but capitalized, in Roman letters, refers to the Western Wall)[17]

Interestingly, in classical times, around the time of the *Hasmonean* dynasty, there were many blurred edges around the issue of who was, or was not a Jew. Of course, this is not to project onto that time the modern concept of 'identity crisis,' as the culture would not have had such a form of ego-development, or evolved an 'ego-consciousness' in the modern sense as the Austrian philosopher Rudolf Steiner puts it.[18] Yet *Midrashic* texts refer to difficulties in identifying whether someone was a Jew or not, as gentiles could mix with those identified as Jews and even observe the customs including attending synagogue. Sometimes gentiles were taken for Jews (therefore were Jews for practical purposes) by pretending to be so or converted often to avail themselves of situations where being a Jew conferred certain privileges:

> *'Some gentiles will have been called Jews, others will have called themselves Jews. In situations where status as a Jew conferred privilege, and/or esteem, the status will have been coveted by outsiders, and we may be sure that as a result some Jews converted to Judaism and others simply declared themselves to be Jews.'* [19]

Later, rabbinic Judaism tightened up the loopholes and developed a matrilineal rule regarding legal status as a Jew after much Rabbinic debate from the 2nd Century C.E. onward. But issues remained and intensified after the creation of the State of Israel and the formation of a notional ethno-national entity.[20] The issue of what constituted Jewish identity was considered of such central importance by David Ben Gurion that in 1958 he initiated a great debate about it, inviting fifty leading Jewish intellectuals to

---

17 Ibid.
18 Rudolf Steiner, The Christ Impulse and the Development of Ego-Consciousness, pp. 95-111
19 Shaye J. Cohen, *The Beginnings of Jewishness,* p. 68.
20 Ibid. Pp. 263-307

respond to a number of issues the State faced regarding balancing freedom of conscience against religious stipulations; the meaning of 'nation' in relation to 'religion;' the implicit discriminatory nature of 'the law of return;' and the need to integrate Jews of varied cultural backgrounds while trying to 'increase shared and unifying properties.'[21] The matter of what to do about the status of mixed marriages was also pressing:

> 'As Israel declared itself a Jewish state, the definition of Jewish identity now became an open legal issue with critical implications. It would determine the way in which a citizen's national allegiance was indicated on the official identity card, who was entitled to Israeli citizenship, who would receive the financial assistance offered new immigrants, and even application for marriage license. The Law of Return which grants Israeli citizenship to any Jew wishing to settle in the country, similarly required a clear operative definition of Jewish identity.'[22]

Ben Gurion's emphasis on forcing some sort of unity out of the extraordinary mix of cultures and traditions was not only pressing but threw into relief how vulnerable and changeable identity could be:

> 'the self-image it conveys, the risks of social fracture that it carries, its imaginary dimension, its evident dependence on others, and ones capacity or inability to change it.'[23]

Ben Gurion was largely concerned about identity in a legalistic sense which is yet another category of identity but not entirely separated from the issue of psychological identification we are largely dealing with in this chapter. These separate notions of identity intersect with each other. Identity, whether in a legal or psychological sense also relies on creating boundaries, an 'us and them.' And although liberal notions of tolerant co-existence and the evolution of so-called multiculturalism have posited the 'rainbow' of identities working in a collegiate manner, questions

---

21   Eliezar Ben-Rafael, *Jewish Identities, Fifty Intellectuals answer Ben Gurion,* p. 146.

22   Ibid, P. 32

23   Shlomo Sand, *How I stopped Being a Jew,* p. 9.

are still raised around whether identity, as such, creates barriers to communication and interaction and indeed, whether 'tolerance' is the best we can do, although unquestionably preferable to outright conflict of course. Identity is of course the product of thought and its external manifestation as language. Language, as Nietzsche put it, can catch us in its 'net' and control, unwittingly, the direction of our thinking. Gilad Atzmon makes this point effectively, notwithstanding the occasional characteristic hint of acerbity:

> 'The statement: 'I look into myself and see a Zionist, a gay, a woman, a nation, a watermelon,' and so on, means: I identify with Zionism, gays, women, certain politics and so on. Once we think we are already defeated by the dictatorial power of language. Marginal communities and identity political discourses are generally very sensitive to the power of language and this is probably the reason why a substantial amount of marginal political effort is dedicated to imposing lingual restriction...usually in the name of political correctness, liberalism and even tolerance.'[24]

Rabbinical Judaism's traditions of *Mishnaic*, *Talmudic* and *Aggadic* exegesis place language and its *polysemic* nature at the forefront of our awareness. The endless recycling of debate in Orthodox, Jewish tradition is itself an insight into the fundamental difficulties of seeing language and the images it creates as firm ground that we can take for granted despite the core of observances around which this debate circles. The longing for a state of being where language becomes clear, solid, unambiguous and indubitably truthful is, not surprisingly, a part of the anticipated messianic age until which point we battle with 'stubborn words.'[25] In this respect, Judaism's own traditions question the notion of easy identity by constantly asking about its presuppositions. If there is a form of identity connected with a religion centred on questioning that very thing then the abandonment of that religion and adoption of a secular life generates an intensification of identity issues. But does this leave Jews in as dire a situation as the one Gilad Atzmon describes where

---

24   Gilad Atzmon, *The Wandering Who*, p. 36.
25   See: Umberto Eco, *The Search for the Perfect Language*.

'what remains of Jewish identity is pretty threadbare. Once stripped of religious spirituality, all that is left of Jewish-ness is a template of negation fuelled by racial orientation and spiced up with some light cultural references such as matzo balls and chicken soup.' [26]

Atzmon's assertion is, perhaps, particularly polarised and stretched while containing some kernel of truth. It's generally unlikely that Orthodox Jews saw themselves as having an 'identity' in the modern sense of the word where a self-image is prevalent. Orthodox Jews, it seems to me, see themselves as primarily a religious group and do not have any truck with the identity issues of more recent years. In this respect, it could be seen as 'non-identitarian' although externally identifiable. In modern Israel, of course, there are, indeed, forms of strong identitarian Jews who consider themselves Orthodox, we've already mentioned the settler movement with its attendant visuals: long hair, swaddled in *Talesim*[27] against which automatic rifles swing. This creates a powerful image, almost a fashion statement, similar to secular Jews who adopt orthodoxy, the *Baalei Teshuvah*,[28] who, as we have seen, might be keen to display their new found identity through demonstrative visuals. Identity often needs these visual signifiers that point out you are a member of a club. Even Quakers, perhaps the most image eschewing religious group of all time, have been associated, somewhat satirically with manifesting some sort of identifiable image![29] So even by pairing down external symbols, as in the case of the Quakers, who meet in buildings shorn, as much as possible, of visual signifiers and who, in their early days especially, simplified their manner of dress, can still create a vestigial image that could, potentially be identarian. The attempt to discard the 'mask' creates another 'mask.'

---

26   Gilad Atzmon, Op. Cit. p. 55

27   TALLIT (Heb. יִת‎ ל‏‏ טַ, pl. *tallitot*; Yid. *tales*, pl. *talesim*), prayer shawl. Originally the word meant "gown" or "cloak." This was a rectangular mantle that looked like a blanket and was worn by men in ancient times. At the four corners of the *tallit* tassels were attached in fulfillment of the biblical commandment of ẓiẓit (Num. 15:38–41). https://www.jewishvirtuallibrary.org/tallit

28   https://en.wikipedia.org/wiki/Baal_teshuva

29   'However, sometimes it comes up in conversation that British Quakers today, having mostly left behind plain dress and certainly the strict dress codes which sometimes went with it, nevertheless still have some distinctive ways of dressing. We joke about the socks-with-sandals and the anything-accessorised-by-Guardian.' https://brigidfoxandbuddha.wordpress.com/2014/01/03/search-terms-quaker-dress/

In a recent interview on the *Katie Halper Show*[30], Norman Finkelstein, whose political views are undeniably radical and left-leaning, affirmed his identity as a Jew when a viewer's question was forwarded to him that stated you probably could not be a Jew as an atheist and secular person (which is how Finkelstein has described himself). His response is as follows:

> *Finkelstein: That's ridiculous!*
>
> *Halper: it's a meshegas!*
>
> *Finkelstein: If I went before a group of people and announced 'I'm not Jewish' – Finkelstein!?? Your gestures; your intonations; you're like Woody Allen and you're not Jewish!??*
>
> *Halper: It's like they said 'Bernie [Bernie Sanders] was hiding it,' how can you hide it, for whom?*
>
> *Finkelstein: Yeh, it's a stupid thing to say, so, you know Hannah Arendt put it, she said 'being Jewish is one of the objective givens of my life,' and then the question is what you choose to do with that fact -but it's an objective given.*

This is in stark contrast to Atzmon's notion of desperately hanging on to 'matzo balls and chicken soup' as last ditch cultural signifiers and raises the question of more deeply rooted cultural realities, although a recent cultural and inter-faith exchange in the UK between Jewish and Muslim groups called the '*chicken soup challenge*' might have encouraged one to think otherwise, affirming, as it does at least in a titular sense, Atzmon's more minimal view of the remnants of identity once Orthodoxy

---

30 https://www.youtube.com/watch?v=bMUDf5oBdx0 The relevant part of the interview start at approx. 34.13.

is eschewed.[31] Halper's interjection of *"it's a Meshegas,"* sounds almost a performative reference to a remnant of a 'Yiddishism,' another signifier thrown in as a sort of identity affirmation but without, perhaps, the strength of Finkelstein's claim to belong to a world of gestural, intonational and nominatively determined Jewishness due, perhaps partly, to a generational difference and parental inheritances from the pre-war world. Finkelstein's background, as the son of East European refugees who were also part of the Jewish, Eastern European intellectual milieu, gives him a direct connection to that rich but lost world of Jewish modernism that thrived before the horrors descended. For the next generation of Jews, this connection would be weaker and the sense of identity more questionable, specifically for those that did not don the garb of the new Jewish ethno-nationalism we have discussed. Clearly, Finkelstein's sense of his Jewishness being an 'objective given' runs counter to Atzmon's view that 'assimilated or secular Jews would find it hard to list any particular positive quality that may identify them as Jews.'[32] For Finkelstein, it seems, the sense of being a Jew is rich enough in signifiers, although his reference to New York Jewishness via the Woody Allen comparison might indicate that there is a geographical element to ease of identity. Growing up in the North of England, perhaps, does not lend itself quite so readily to that ease. Yet, historically, there has been an ambivalence about being identified as Jewish amongst secular Jews as this well known joke exemplifies:

> 'If you want to complement a Jew...tell him that he does not look like one. What a depth of degradation for a people to have reached,' observed the Anglo-Jewish writer Israel Zangwill in 1904. Fifty years later, a popular joke among American Jews reveals the persistent preoccupation with the question of Jewish looks. In the joke, an older woman approaches a "dignified" looking gentleman on the subway and

---

31 https://www.eastlondonadvertiser.co.uk/news/mitzvah-day-challenge-making-jewish-chicken-soup-at-east-london-3613408 Worth noting that it turned out that this event had specific political backing that raised questions about its good faith in being purely an inter-faith event given that it 'was also backed by the UK Home Office, through a programme that provides funding and support for counter-extremism projects, a detail that went unmentioned in reports produced by BBC News and The Guardian..'

32 Gilad Atzmon. op. Cit. p. 61.

proceeds to unmask what she suspects are his ethnic origins. "Pardon me for asking." she inquires, "but are you Jewish?" He coldly replies, "No," he is not Jewish. A few minutes later she asks again. "Are you sure you are not Jewish?" And he repeats that he is definitely sure. But the woman is not convinced, and she approaches him a third time. "Are you absolutely sure you are not Jewish?" Finally , he breaks down and confesses, "All right. All right, I am Jewish." "That's funny," remarks the woman. "You don't look Jewish."[33]

In her essay which relates the above 'joke,' Susan A. Glenn, writes of the gradual shift from ambivalence around what might be identifiable Jewish characteristics to a more positive acknowledgement of them, as in the case of the Finkelstein example. Positive in the sense that they are an objective reality as claimed by Finkelstein and also positive in the sense of taking pride in a so-called 'ethnic identity' which latter is a phenomenon linked to Zionism, in turn part of the surge in identity culture in the last forty years. Finkelstein, it is worth pointing out, has made it clear he is not only not interested in identity culture but considers it an aberration on the part of Left to have espoused it.[34] Glenn sees three phases in the development of Jewish attitudes to the notion of physical identifiers: from 1910 to the end of World War Two, where anthropologists like Franz Boas focused away from the dominant biological determinants, so disastrously popular at the time, to cultural and environmental factors, seeing Jews as no different, essentially, to the cultures in which they lived; from 1940's to 1960's,

when psychological experts -many of whom were Jews-took over the field of anti-race science, Jewish and non-Jewish psychologists would make even bolder claims, insisting not only that Jews were virtually indistinguishable from non-Jews but that anyone who

33 Susan A. Glenn, *"That's Funny You Don't Look Jewish,." Visual Stereotypes and the Making of Modern Jewish Identity. In Boundaries of Jewish Identity,* p. 64.
34 See: https://www.youtube.com/watch?v=2PxUdhRGQkk

believed otherwise was probably racist at best, at worst
a proto-fascist[35]

and a third period, the last fifty years, 'when Jews found greater social acceptance and when groups promoting racial and ethnic pride began dominating American culture.'[36] As we have noted, post 67/73 gradually increased the connection between Zionism and Jewish identity and the concomitant ethno-nationalism exemplified by Israeli politicians such as Itamar Ben Gvir and Bezalel Smotrich today, are positions diametrically and vociferously opposed to the notion of a Jewishness that equivocates around identity. Compare this to the writer Bruno Schulz, who 'developed his extraordinary imagination in a swarm of identities and nationalities; he was a Jew who thought and wrote in Polish, was fluent in German, immersed in Jewish culture, yet unfamiliar with the Yiddish language.'[37] Yet, to hark back to this vital but lost world and culture,

> *'to collect documents, factual accounts, and all sorts of*
> *material in order to keep alive the traditions and the*
> *history. This artificial respiration...would no longer*
> *bring back the breath and the pulse of life into the*
> *dead body.'*[38]

So where does this leave the Jewish person who cannot totally resuscitate that 'lost world' other than desperately ply his imaginary bellows to the fading embers and yet who cannot hang their hat on the hatstand of ethno-nationalism?

For people of 'Jewish background'[39] like myself, the lack of direct connection to Eastern European/European forebears (my grandmother, probably from Kovno/Kaunas died before I was born) can create a sense of fluidity and instability around identity. My envy of Asian friends, when I was a young man, who had inherited a language from their parental background was based on a rather simplistic notion that a shared language

---

35   Susan A. Glenn, Op, Cit. p. 66-67.

36   Ibid.

37   "Who Owns Bruno Schulz?" Archived October 8, 2007, at the Wayback Machine, by Benjamin Palof Boston Review (December 2004/January 2005).

38   Isaac Deutscher, *The Non-Jewish Jew*, p. 1

39   My choice of describing myself 'of Jewish background' is itself an expression of some degree of havering around identity.

handed identity to you on a plate. I felt bereft that I had not inherited this bilingualism. By the '80's, as multiculturalism started taking off and an industry was spawned which was arguably neo-colonial in nature, I became aware of Asian friends in the world of arts suddenly finding that their cultural background could become 'currency' and a distinct advantage. Some friends were very free and open in telling me they were '*playing the ethnic card*' to enhance their prospects. So I was envious yet again – how come I couldn't massage my Jewish background into a portable identity that could be seen as 'colourful' and 'exotic' in some similar way? During this time, David Baddiel's temporally displaced notion of '*Jews Don't Count*' might have had some real meaning but he used it nearly forty years later when it was a manifest absurdity to say such a thing. As British Society is now going through a sort of 'blowback' experience to that very form of multiculturalism that became known as 'woke,' only to be replaced by another form of inverted 'wokeism' that pushed populist, identarian politics, the '*new Jew*' identity, as we have explored, fitted comfortably with this political agenda. Baddiel was decades late with his supposed critique which stank of irrelevance and staleness as he proclaimed it.

Now, the old 'woke' became replaced by a 'new woke' which attempted to posit itself as more 'commonsensical,' more authentic and more 'naturalistic' allying itself to a brusque and callousing economics that mocked anything that appeared flakey or vulnerable in anyway. It seems that the Left's espousal of multiculturalism and identity politics delivered its own karmic consequences. To some degree the Corbyn and Bernie Sanders years returned the left to a more class conscious base, focused on changing the neoliberal, economic ideology which was why the vested interests of the establishment had to pull every stop out to destroy it, some of those stops carrying within them, no doubt, the seeds of further blowback. Populism and majority identarianism was used as a vehicle to crush this potent call for change.

As we have noted, the contrasting pictures on the front of this book again serve to illustrate the change. In the lower, contemporary picture, the identification is about flags: the flag of the 'new Jewish' ethno-nationalism combined with the populism of the United Kingdom. The message being sent is 'we are ethno-nationalist Jews and as such are allies with the populist movement of the UK, in this we are loyal to both.' The picture above is about fighting fascism and is part of an international movement of the Left to combat nationalist authoritarianism. They show Jewish people expressing diametrically opposed views of the world. The universal against the essentialist stance. The mainstream part of the Jewish communities was now propping up a Government that was anti-immigrant, using some of the most flagrantly cliched jingoistic language available that came across, to anybody not caught up in it, as cheap pastiche withered and stale at its utterance. As Shlomo Sand has observed '[i]t was hard to deny a glaring reality: the development of an essentialist, non-religious identity encourages the perpetuation of ethnocentric, racist or quasi-racist positions, both in Israel and abroad.'[40]

The post '67/'73 evolution of the new nationalist Jewish identity and its 'fictional creation of ethnic unity,'[41] at least amongst the mainstream part of the communities (which has become the public view of Jews in the UK via its official institutions) has now reached its zenith or nadir depending on where you are positioned amongst the Jewish communities. It seems something to lament, this loss of the universalist Jew, fraught with the psychological insecurity of identity that possibly fuelled that universalism. Is this no more than a sentimental construct on my part, a nostalgia trip without any of the real and potent risks taken by those that actually lived that life? To some degree, yes and the nostalgic resuscitations of Yiddish by Jews on the Left, like myself, are perhaps partaking of this conjuring of images of the past to which their connection is limited. The ten million Yiddish speakers living before World War Two are now only a few hundred thousand at most, largely concentrated within New York's Chassidic communities.[42] So, perhaps

> *'[t]he rich Yiddish culture is now extinct. It's true that some students take classes in the language of the*

---

40   Shlomo Sand, op. Cit. p. 7.

41   Op Cit. p. 48. *'Secular Zionism deeply internalised both the religious myth of Abrahamic descent and the Christian legend of the accursed and wandering people condemned to exile for their sins. On the basis of these two matrixes, it succeeded in fashioning the image of an ethnic group whose palpably fictional character (one need only observe the diversity of appearance of Israelis) in no way subtracted from its effectiveness.'* Note the phrase 'fashioning the image.' Image formation and its psychological/emotional value plays a significant role in identity formation which can take many forms including the self image of being a universalist and non-identarian if it functions in an identity based way,

42   See: https://www.youtube.com/watch?v=Dl856YM_krU

Eastern European Jews, but they do not communicate or create in this langugae. Linguistic study and the connection with Yiddish culture may warm the hearts of nostalgists, but they cannot possibly create characters and situations like those encountered in the literary monuments bequeathed by such writers as Shalom Aleichem or Isaac Bashevis Singer.' [43]

It seems all avenues towards creating a Jewish culture via the very questioning of identity are now closed. Ethno-nationalism has won the day it seems. This leaves Jews who reject ethno-nationalism and religious observance potentially with identity issues if these arise at all as many people are just doing their best to cope with the exigences of their daily lives. But as I have tried to argue, the questioning of identity, feeling unsure of identity, feeling the psychological ground under one's feet as not always secure and working creatively with that might well have a vital role to play in countering what we see emerging around us today. The less hatstands to hang your hat on the better! The more we drop the obsession with the easy psychological security that identity offers us the better!

This is, of course, all pie in the sky stuff redolent of the most armchair fixated philosopher. Obsession with identity and 'roots' has afflicted us with awful manifestations from the effulgent emotionalism of television programs where the new DNA technology allowed people to discover apparent aspects of their ancestry causing them to breakdown in tears in front of the ready cameras, as if something timeless and essential about that individual were being revealed; to the more recent insistence that DNA tests prove ancestors were living in the Israel of the *Hasmoneans* thus trumping all Palestinian rights, despite the fact that DNA science advances 'have not managed to characterise a Jew on the basis of the DNA genotype.' [44] This seems to be another phase of trying to find some sort of psychological security through apparent 'scientific' proofs in order to be able to rest easy about the issue and put ethnicity issues to bed resting on the laurels of 'knowing who one is.' But there are, as Susan Martha Kahn points out, trenchant issues connected with this approach:

---

43 Shlomo Sand, op. Cit. p. 40 et seq.
44 Shlomo Sand, op. Cit. p. 79.

'The consequences of the Jewish embrace of new genetic technologies are uncertain: will Jews cede authority to determine Jewishness to technological methods – interpreted through, but ultimately detached from, Jewish tradition? Will traditional practices for reckoning Jewish identity be abandoned? Perhaps the Jewish embrace of these technologies simply amplifies an ambiguity about Jewish identity that has been a constant of Jewish history – for Jewish identity has always been simultaneously fixed and fluid...[i]s an identity that is conceptualised as shifting and complex less real than an identity that is reified in genetic terms?' [45]

In a world saturated in identity issues, as so many people, understandably rendered insecure by a faceless globalist capitalism and its wealth siphoning, try to grasp onto something that appears to offer meaning, the 'new Jewish identity' is flying high. Who wants the 'old Jew' with the prevarications over identity and the soul searching when you can have absolute certainty about who you are? No more slandering of Josef K. Old Josef can now stick his chest out and march with pride waving the flag of his ethno-nationalism. Is this now the death of the 'universalist Jew' who sees in her/his identity issues a call to something broader than psychological identification?

Shlomo Sand, questions whether there really was any 'universalistic' tradition to Judaism seeing much of Jewish religious tradition such as 'love they neighbour as thyself' as an 'intragroup morality' rather than a universalist call.[46] Answering the obvious question of why there has been an extraordinarily significant number of people of Jewish origin who manifested this universalism such as 'Karl Marx, Leon Trotsky, Rosa Luxemburg, Kurt Eisner, Carlo Rosselli, Léon Blum, Otto Bauer, Pierre Mendes-France, Abraham Sarfati, Daniel Cohn-Bendit, Noam Chomsky, Daniel Bensaid, Naomi Klein...'[47] Sands explains this as a combination of the enlightenment influencing the loosening of religious ties combined with the collective memory of oppression:

---

45   Susan Martha Kahn, *Are Genes Jewish?* In *Boundaries of Jewish Identity*, p. 23.

46   Shlomo Sand, op. Cit. p. 70

47   Ibid. P. 73.

'The distancing of these individuals, and so many more, from the Jewish religious tradition was inversely proportional to their convergence with a humanist view of the world and a burning desire to change the conditions of people's lives, whoever those people might be, and not just members of their own religion, their own community or their own nation.' [48]

The memory of oppression, according to Sands, allowed Jews, in particular to empathise with the other forms of oppression created by social and economic ideologies as well as other forms of racially based injustice.

'The oppression exercised by the dominant religious civilisations towards a religious minority prepared the ground so that, with the advent of the Enlightenment, a section of the oppressed joined, in the course of their secularisation, with all those who suffered, proclaiming solidarity with them.' [49]

Sands hints at the possibility that some memory of the salvific and redemptive features of Judaism might have played a part in this development as well. There is also the notion that Jews were to be 'a light unto the nations' as expounded in the Prophet Isaiah (42.6), although this has overtones of 'chosenness' and essentialism it nevertheless expresses something more than a purely 'intra-group morality.' Immanuel Jakobovits, the last Chief Rabbi (he ceded office in 1991) to vociferously critique aspects of Israeli policy and speak out strongly for justice for Palestinians, in contrast to Sands, does assert that there is a universalist message in Judaism. In a talk delivered in 1972 addressing the murder of Israeli athletes at the Munich Olympics he declared that

[o]ur prophets would have emphasised particularly the moral call to share in the ordeal of others, as we want others to share in ours. It has always been the Jewish characteristic that our compassion extends to all who suffer, even our enemies. Our sages tell us that the

---

48   Ibid. P. 73.
49   Ibid. P. 73-74.

hundred notes of the Shofar which we sound on the New Year are meant to echo the hundred sighs that rose from the bereaved mother of Sisera, when he was slain in his battle against the Jewish people in Biblical times.[50]

Whatever the truth here, it seems as if the period of Jewish universalism is petering out in conjunction with the rise of a form of collective, Jewish, ethno-nationalist identity that runs counter to it. The rise of Israel as 'the collective Jew' has forced the concept of an *ethnos-based* nationality and an ossified form of identification upon people of Jewish background inclining non-Jews to see Jews in terms of Zionism and the Middle East regardless of individual stances, indifference, or groups that are part of the Jewish communities that disavow this. The so-called *'clash of civilisations'* that has thrown out cheap, binary indentarianism pitting a fictional monolithic Islam against an equally fictional monolith West has strengthened the notion that the State of Israel is a bulwark against 'the barbarian hoard.' This harks back to Herzl's statement that settlers in Palestine would form a '"rampart of Europe against Asia," and "an outpost of civilization as opposed to barbarism."'[51] These simplistic binary juxtapositions, that seem to strengthen an 'us and them,' that can fortify a form of psychological security through identity as we have already discussed in relation to the Brexit/Remain oppositional pair in the UK, are also extremely dangerous, divisive and destructive, allowing forces of economic power to disguise themselves as 'moral quests.' This tendency to see the Israel/Palestine conflict in this light (or perhaps in 'this darkness') takes the focus off the underlying reality of the conflict being between Israelis and Palestinians and the struggle for territorial and economic control. This has been pointed out by prominent anti-Zionist Rabbi Yaakov Shapiro.[52]

'It's not Islam and its not Muslims against Jews, that's the main thing we have to tell people. It's a political thing, its Israel its not the Jews. They like to conflate it because, this way, number one, they get the support

---

50   Jakobovits, *If Only My People…Zionism in My Life,* p. 191
51   https://learninglink.oup.com/access/content/von-sivers-3e-dashboard-resources/document-excerpts-from-theodor-herzl-the-jewish-state-1895
52   Interview with Rabbi Shapiro: https://www.youtube.com/watch?v=QKRSiqBWqNM

*of the Evangelicals, number two, its very easy to say,
if your are a Palestinian, "you're an antisemite"...it's a
political conflict between Israel and the Palestinians it
has nothing to do with the Jews being Jews it has nothing
to do with Muslims...I mean how many Palestinians are
observant Muslims?...'*

Whether what we call Jewishness was at its most creative as an anti-identarian force is, of course, a moot point. Dilemmas of identity do seem to be more conducive to asking questions about what constitutes identity and might well help inoculate ourselves against its worst manifestations. There has been much reference to 'sovereignty' in recent years as countries have become increasingly concerned about the effects of globalism on democracy, particularly in the EU where 'democratic deficits' are referred to. These manifestations have been particularly fertile for the populist Right who are adept at turning concerns about democracy and economic sovereignty into identity issues. 'Sovereignty' is not, inherently about nationalistic fervour, however, rather, it is a term used to denote national control over economic, democratic and currency matters. It need not be used to create the stale and retro identity issues such as *'make America great again'* or the penchant in the UK for prefixing newly created institutions with *'Great British.'* Johnson tried to do this with a failing and significantly foreign-owned privatised rail network and Starmer is now imitating it in his characteristically vacuous manner with the notion of a renewable energy agency called *'Great British Energy,'* in the hope of desperately humouring Brexit voters. Whether these grotesquely forced references to past notions of 'greatness,' that have nothing to do with the geographical meaning of *'great,'* will continue to hallucinate elements in the electorate remains to be seen. The notion of sovereignty, therefore, need not presage some sort of return to nation states trying to regain the so-called pomp, splendour and flag-waving of the past but rather a returning of democracy and currency control (as in the case of the Eurozone) so as to be able to look after its people better. This does not negate the possibility of a universalism that improves human communication and the furtherance of a social transformation that promotes equity in terms of access to resources and psychological well-being.

Maybe we should see the positives in indentity dilemmas around nationality and ethnicity. According to Gilad Atzmon, nationality is a 'phantasmal narrative,' and '[a]nthropological and historical studies of different so-called 'peoples' and 'nations' lead, embarrassingly, to the crumbling of every ethnicity and ethnic identity.'[53] If this is true then some serious questions around these issues are in order. The asking of the questions that Jewish crises of identity have brought up, seems to have dried up, largely. We seem, now, to be in the grip of a disquieting search for security through identity, the 'woke' identity being the other side of the coin of the 'anti-woke' identity, each claiming to be 'truth' and 'common sense.' Doubt and questioning retreats as:

> *each human being seeks psychological security, inward security, relying on belief, holding on, hoping thereby in a belief to find security, in an ideal, in a person, in a concept, in an experience and does he[sic] ever find security in any of this? You understand my question? And if he doesn't, why does he hold on to them? You understand my question?* [54]

It's important here that a short coda is added. The armchair philosophising of this chapter might well have fallen into the trap that Gary Saul Morson points out is a common feature of adopting a moralising tone in relation to deep, psychologically rooted human issues. He points out that

> *'One might naively think that the more important the moral question, the more responsible the analysis would be; but in practice, the more serious the charge, the greater the temptation to crude moral posturing.'*[55]

It's obviously easy for me, someone not significantly oppressed, or against whom grave and serious injustices have not, by and large, been committed (except for the economic ones we have discussed) to raise questions around the psychology of identity and the value of psychological insecurity around the same. Yet identity can, perhaps, be of value when

---

53   Gilad Atzmon, *The Wandering Who*, p. 136

54   https://jkrishnamurti.org/content/there-security-all-psychologically#:~:text=-So%20we%20are%20saying%3A%20there,form%20of%20relationship%20as%20 attachment.

55   Gary Saul Morson, *Apologetics and negative Apologetics, in People of the Book* ed. Rubin-Dorsky and Fishkin, p. 82.

it forms around issues of injustice, particularly offences against those that consider themselves to posses 'peoplehood,' often those defined as aboriginal or native to a particular geographical area that has been settler-colonised in some way. The flags of those against whom such injustices have been committed seem softer, like the appeal of an innocent compared to the pomp and bombast of the flags of imperia. In this sort of situation the identity marker of a flag can be a call to solidarity of a disadvantaged group. I was recently watching a video of the ceremonial opening of Gaza airport as part of some research connected with this chapter. I could remember watching it on television back in 1998 and feeling a sort of sadness as the ceremony took place: the flags on the control tower, the band playing '*Men of Harlech*,' the slow, stately march and the soldiers with epaulettes. There was a strange muted quality to all of it, a result of back projecting, perhaps which seemed to echo the latent fragility of the situation. I mused, at that time about the fragile nascency of national identity and the military style appurtenances that seemed a necessary part of its affirmation. Perhaps there was no pragmatic alternative, perhaps, in these situations, a technical form of identity is necessary on the path to self-determination. But something balked, just as the Israeli flag caused me to balk at the manifestation of something that felt, in its nature, to be an echo of the very oppressive forces that shaped this response in turn: More flags, more states, more borders, more us and them, more fight for resources, more wealth siphoning of land and housing.[56] Three years later, the airport was bombed after the onset of the Second *Intafada* and a year after that completely bulldozed.

---

56   56https://www.dw.com/en/real-estate-market-booms-in-gaza/a-15226449

Postscript

This short book has covered a wide range of issues that I felt moved in parallel to the so-called 'Labour antisemitism crisis.' I have also considered other issues that, whilst not connecting directly with the antisemitism issue, echo some of its structural features. During the writing of this book, I constantly asked myself the question 'what is the purpose of doing this? Isn't it a futile exercise in trying to challenge a narrative that has already ossified into a seemingly unassailable truth?' I'm not an academic and not really a writer as such yet, at the same time, there was some need to get a voice 'out there' to challenge the fast drying layer of weatherproof paint that was hardening on the events of 2015 to the present and that was forming a fixed truth narrative. Behind this hardened protective covering there were and are the voices of those shocked by one of the most disturbing attempts in modern times to destroy democracy and maintain the control of hegemonic vested interests at a geo-political as well as national level. These voices need to be heard as that period is in the process of being painted over by our political class, so that even the memory of the attempt at change is to be expunged. So, inexpertly equipped as I am, I felt an obligation to shout out as the fast drying paint was being thickly applied despite the sense that in the near future one may be left shouting in some sort of anechoic chamber. Whether we are left shouting in that anechoic booth is dependent upon individuals to keep the challenge to the official narrative alive. This book, as miniscule in its impact as it will be, is a small contribution to that effort. Of course, others much more skilled than myself and with more of a public profile have challenged these dominant narratives and have done it in a significantly more effective way than this book has done. Indeed, some of them are quoted in this book. Nevertheless, due to the marginalisation of these people and their lack of appearances in the mainstream media, I felt it worthwhile to add another Jewish voice that might, with other voices added, raise the volume slightly above that of a whisper. If 0dB is near silence then we need to get to around 60dB which is considered conversational level.

'As of November 23rd, 2021, there have been 2,465,286 new book titles published this year' proclaimed a website that provides data on book publishing worldwide. Can there be any point in adding another one in a world already glutted? Perhaps not. After all, we have earlier referred to the plethora of books on economics that appeared after the banking collapse of 2008 which explained again and again how the banking system has sucked wealth out of economies, created asset bubbles and destroyed communities and lives. Yet electorates have seemed keen to keep propping it up, digesting the disinformation delivered to them by actors who themselves, whilst being part of the financial system promise liberation from the issues it has created. Do books have any real impact on already ossified views and the dynamics at work in our society? Probably very little or often non.

The palpable futility should be a powerful disincentive and if anything, encourage a sort of Zen-like taciturnity whilst the 'gross blunders of history' play themselves out. Yet there is something in the human breast that wants to speak out and even holler against manifest injustice especially at a time when egregious lies are delivered, not only in a barefaced fashion, but with a glib smugness and sense of self-satisfaction that they can be knowingly delivered with total impunity. Whether there is a slow fuse burning that will bring a decisive reaction to this, as geo-political commentator Alexander Mercouris opines[1], is very unclear at present. It's certainly unclear in the UK, where a bizarre docility and almost limitless tolerance of mendacity and scam seems to be the norm. I have already tried to offer some explanations for this but still wonder whether there are boundaries to its sustainability. Perhaps the exigences of financialisation have so shaped our world of thought and feeling that there is doubt that change is possible or fear that change may bring something worse.

I have also argued that the leverage of antisemitism for cheap political purposes, whilst connected with geo-political issues of some note, was, essentially, part and parcel of the creation of a decoy and general distraction mechanism in order to take the spotlight off the underlying issues that exposed the mechanisms of the wealth-siphoning vested interests. Economist, Richard Wolff, in one of his recent 'Global Capitalism'

---

1   https://www.youtube.com/watch?v=h2c3pfGSjtc

videos describes this issue of distraction very directly and succinctly and it bears quoting him at length:

> 'The British came up with a way of deflecting the anger of their working class which was more extreme...because the British working class, particularly after 2008, was really heavily damaged by the austerity programs... and by the inability of the Labour movement, except for the short period of Mr. Corbyn, to be much of an opposition... and so they had to come up with an extreme distraction, they did -it's called Brexit. They convinced the British people... your problem is the Europeans, we should split...they did; the British economy has been going down ever since...it solved nothing. It gave Mr. Boris Johnson, a naughty boy with bad hair [a chance] to become famous because he galvanised a bitter working class's desire for something to change...there was nothing there...there was no policy and...Mr. Johnson leaves as befuddled and irrelevant to what's going on. Indeed, his parting shot will, in the future, be understood, not to be lying to the British people about the contempt he holds them in but rather his excited embrace of the war in Ukraine...as a way of distracting people from the reality of the British economy which is an...unmitigated disaster.'[2]

We also need to see the so-called 'antisemitism crisis' in a similar way. The importance the manufactured 'antisemitism crisis' played in creating distraction, diversion and decoy is fulsomely attested to by the recent comments of former Chancellor Nadhim Zahawi who, in July 2022, as part of an encomium (read: stab in the back) to Johnson who was being pressurised to resign at the time, wrote in his letter to him that 'no one will forget getting Brexit done, keeping a dangerous antisemite out of No10.' This comment which went unchallenged by the opposition, including its Jewish M.P's, who were apparently happy to prop up the stale narrative under Starmer's questionable tutelage and remain silent as they witnessed yet more cheap abuse of the term, was a clear indicator of the central role

---

2   Richard Wolff, Global Capitalism, https://www.youtube.com/watch?v=HGVfTS489IY (from c. 26').

in undermining change that the political leverage of antisemitism played. Why would he otherwise have mentioned it so emphatically had it not played such a significant role? The idea that Zahawi had a particular interest or concern about real antisemitism and the Jewish communities seems a far fetched notion. It was clearly another 'philosemitic' leveraging of the issue.

The use of binary pairs such as Brexit/Remain, woke/anti-woke, Good Jew/Bad Jew, in-work poor/ill and vulnerable benefit claimant, mortgaged/unmortgaged created artificial polarities that have undeniably helped prop up a financial class that did not want to see its vested interests affected, particularly the property owning culture surfing a lucrative housing and land bubble that had developed over the preceding half century. An asset bubble which personally benefited them so handsomely whilst gutting the real economy, destroying communities and creating immense stresses on millions of people, not to mention depriving so many of our young people of any sense of a sustainable future. As I type, there is another polarity, that emerging out of the arguably 'proxy war' in Ukraine, a tragedy that expresses itself in another binary of U.S, U.K., E.U./Russia, China, India, Africa. This time it is a grotesque distraction that is causing immense suffering and destruction on a larger scale, although the recent report published in the UK *Journal of Epidemiology and Community Health*,[3] that austerity policies over the last ten years have caused over 330,000 'excess deaths,' raises the question of whether economic policies can be more destructive than actual wars. In reality, the two are related. The austerity policies, an ideological choice and in no way a fiscal necessity, have been a form of war on the population by forcing people to become financialised or suffer marginalisation. The fact that reports like the one published in the *Journal of Epidemiology and Community Health* as well as a series of earlier reports from the UN's *Special Raporteur on Human Rights and Extreme Poverty*, that described the devastating effects of austerity in UK communities,[4] created very little national impact is itself testimony to the fragmentation that the economic ideology of financialisation has created. Any attempt to counter it was

---

3   https://www.theguardian.com/business/2022/oct/05/over-330000-excess-deaths-in-great-britain-linked-to-austerity-finds-study

4   https://www.bristol.ac.uk/poverty-institute/news/2019/un-rapporteur-final-report.html

illiterately labelled 'Marxism'[5] or liberal 'wokism' that fed the decoy of a 'culture war' that the financialised class condescendingly ratcheted up as an opiate. Everything was about maintaining this financialisation of the human being. The term *'financialisation,'* which I have been using repeatedly, is often seen as vague term but can be accurately defined:

> *Financialization is a process whereby financial markets, financial institutions, and financial elites gain greater influence over economic policy and economic outcomes. Financialization transforms the functioning of economic systems at both the macro and micro levels. Its principal impacts are to (1) elevate the significance of the financial sector relative to the real sector, (2) transfer income from the real sector to the financial sector, and (3) increase income inequality and contribute to wage stagnation. Additionally, there are reasons to believe that financialization may put the economy at risk of debt deflation and prolonged recession. Financialization operates through three different conduits: changes in the structure and operation of financial markets, changes in the behaviour of nonfinancial corporations, and changes in economic policy.[6]*

One of the most pernicious effects of financialisation is to fragment societies into individuals who consciously or subconsciously experience themselves as units of 'maximising self interest.' This process is insidious and slowly transforms a culture by the process of financialisation changing imperatives so that the financial sector becomes the 'tail that is wagging the dog' of the real economy in the form of services available and the everyday quality of our lives not to mention tardy responses to environmental degradation. Those not interested in or not adept at 'maximising self-interest' are in danger of falling by the wayside - becoming those that don't do '*the right thing.*'

I have linked all these things with the so-called 'antisemitism crisis' because, as I have mentioned earlier, it is more revealing to try to analyse

---

5   https://www.theguardian.com/society/2014/feb/03/ministers-savage-un-report-abolition-bedroom-tax

6   https://www.levyinstitute.org/pubs/wp_525.pdf

the whole dynamic rather than focus on one of its features in isolation. Without the social and economic transformation of our culture that the last forty years of financialisation have created, many of these phenomena, including the use of antisemitism as a political tool would not have been so easily possible I suspect. The fragmentation and disintegration of social cohesion and the loss of belief that change is at all possible via shift of ideology, is illustrated by this cameo from the Newcastle Mayoral election of 2019 where the Left leaning candidate has to confront, at times, a miasma of indifference:

> *Yet what can't be easily fixed is the chasm between politicians, however new and imaginative, and an electorate that no longer cares. Take Driscoll's canvassing in the Northumberland coastal town of Newbiggin. On an estate of small houses with outdoor benches and garden statuettes, the constant refrain is, "I don't follow politics." When he gamely talks policy, the reply comes, "I'm not getting into that." The contrast between the polite conviction on one side of the door and the bafflement on the other makes modern political activism resemble the Jehovah's Witnesses.*
>
> *This swathe of the electoral map runs blood-red Labour, yet as one canvasser, Jamie, observes: "Policy doesn't matter here. They've forgotten what government can do."* [7]

The subtitle of this book, '*A Lament*,' refers, specifically to the tragic loss of social purpose, social justice and humanistic concern that has occurred within the mainstream of the Jewish communities and whilst I have focussed on this it can, in no way, be seen as divorced from the social and economic factors operating at large as in the above reportage from the Newcastle election. We can broadly say, as the *Media Reform Coalition* stated regarding the antisemitism smears, that there has not only been a 'disinformation paradigm' in this respect but an overarching one. The Brexit/Remain artificially created and inflated culture war was premised

---

7 https://www.theguardian.com/commentisfree/2019/apr/19/newcastle-radical-metro-mayor-corbynista

on an avoidance of any genuine analysis of what the real problems were with the structure of the E.U and the currency set up of the Eurozone. Instead, in order for it to function as a decoy it had to be framed as an identarian issue: on the one hand a bogus notion of a return to a *'Great British' something or other* and on the other hand a campaign to preserve a faux cosmopolitanism that regarded itself as liberal and progressive whilst simultaneously being totally incapable of looking at the ideological structures of the austerity inclined E.U. that were not progressive at all. The bad faith on both sides of this banal binary set up was egregious. Particularly so was the narrative produced on the Right, whose representatives were often those embedded in the wealth siphoning of international financial markets themselves whilst posturing as 'anti-globalists.' Nigel Farage, whose father was a City of London stockbroker paraded himself as a *'fag and beer'* man of the people, who falsely claimed that the housing crisis was largely an immigrant problem hiding, conveniently enough, the culpability of the financial sector over many decades[8] in creating this crisis well before immigration became an issue (connected with the Freedom of Movement from the Eastern European countries that had acceded to the E,U.). Farage benefited from the financial industry whilst trying to farm out its negative aggregate effects somewhere else. Yet again, underlying realities were turned on their head to create classic decoy, diversion and distraction. And it largely worked in the manner it was intended to.

Of course, it was this very housing bubble that Farage tried to blame on immigration, that created and hard- wired the very fragmentation that has made any collegial response to our social and political problems so difficult. The individual or family now saw their wealth embodied in the house and land as an ever inflating asset ensuring wealth would be passed onto succeeding generations as more and more people were being shut out. Yet a large part of the Populist movement on the Right has been about the self-righteousness of the property owner and their family who, having toiled with a millstone mortgage, instead of resenting the financial system that took them for that difficult ride, laud it over others, who have either not bought into such a Sisyphean shove up the mountain or who tried and were not able to manage it. It is now impossible to challenge

---

8   See: Phillip Whitehead, *The Writing on the Wall, Britain in the Seventies,* p. 94 which describes the onset of the first wave of the housing bubble as banks realised that land and housing was the next 'Klondike' for them and remains so to this day, alongside private debt issuance.

this hard-wired notion that housing wealth and asset bubbles are the 'keys to the Kingdom' which creates a worrying dynamic that might mean only further decline or even catastrophe could 'clean the slate' that would allow us to pursue an economy that works for all. Indeed, the expression 'clean the slate' is apposite in this context as that was the very term used in the ancient Near East whose economic wisdom included the realisation that debt peonage could destabilise societies. Michael Hudson points this out at the start of his excellent book '..and forgive them their debts,' an exploration of debt cancellation in the Biblical period:

> 'The idea of annulling debts nowadays seems so unthinkable that most economists and many theologians doubt whether the Jubilee Year could have been applied in practice, and indeed on a regular basis. A widespread impression is that the Mosaic debt jubilee was a utopian ideal. However, Assyriologists have traced it to a long tradition of Near Eastern proclamations....[i]nstead of causing crises, these debt jubilees preserved stability in nearly all Near Eastern societies. Economic polarisation, bondage and collapse occurred when such clean slates stopped being proclaimed.' [9]

As the banking system collapsed, it turned out they were the only ones to get debt relief via central banks soaking up the collapsing assets on their 'buyer of last resort' balance sheets. The system was reset and begun again. This became known as 'reverse socialism,' the government stepping in when misallocation and malfeasance created collapse while the public bore the consequences. Social fragmentation, the notion of the individual and family unit as maximiser of self-interest clearly runs counter to acting in the interests of the whole and involves tolerating disabling and destructive effects as long as enough people appear to be benefiting from such a fragmented set up.

This study has lamented the loss of concern over issues of social justice and equity within a significant section of the Jewish communities we have referred to as the 'mainstream.' We have also discussed how the replacement of this by ethnocentric, indentarian foci, has impoverished

---

[9]   Michael Hudson, ...and forgive them their debts. Lending, Foreclosure amd Redemption From Bronze Age Finance to the Jubilee Year. p. ix

the notion of Jewishness in its role in being a challenger to hegemony and vested interests of various sorts. Historian Arno J. Mayer, quoting the American sociologist Thorsten Veblen's concerns about Zionism, makes just this point:

> 'But Veblen's main misgiving [concerning Zionism] was that, by founding their own state and "turning upon themselves," the Jews would cease to contribute "more than an even share to the intellectual life of modern Europe." He considered the Jews to have been, through the ages, "the pioneers, the uneasy guild of pathfinders and iconoclasts in science, scholarship, and institutional change and growth,"...gifted Jews engaged in intellectual "cross-breeding," becoming a "nation of hybrids" and "disturbers of the intellectual peace." Their "intellectual preeminence" came out of an immersion in gentile culture in which they remained "skeptics"; in part because of the "animus with which the community of safe and sane genitles" met them, the Jews played "their part of guidance and incitement" and wound up "in the vanguard of modern inquiry."' [10]

The attempt to destroy and wipe out the "disturbers of the intellectual peace" came over ten years after Veblen's death and this tragedy, in turn, catalysed the process that culminated in the strengthening of the identarianism that has utterly transformed and arguably disfigured the concept of antisemitism as it became a term of geo-political leverage in support of this identarian project. The loss of that central role of "disturbing intellectual peace," which Krishnamurti referred to as "the flame of discontent"[11] seems a terrible loss which manifested itself so profoundly during the UK's only serious bid for a deep change in economic ideology and renewal of social justice. That dominant elements within the mainstream of the Jewish communities contributed to the disabling of

---

10   Arno J. Mayer, *Ploughshares into Swords*, p. 42.

11   See: J. Krishnamurti, The Flame of Discontent https://jkrishnamurti.org/content/ series-iii-chapter-16-flame-discontent *'A man [sic] who is merely satisfied, without understanding the full significance of discontent, is asleep; he is not sensitive to the whole movement of life. Satisfaction is a drug, and it is comparatively easy to find. But to understand the full significance of discontent, the search for certainty must cease.'*

this change is deeply unsettling to me, though, as we have observed, not inherently unique or separated from other social changes that enabled a campaign of disinformation to triumph so spectacularly. What is different is the radical shift from being significant "disturbers of the intellectual peace" to substantially becoming those that sustained the forces of that status quo. That is what the word 'lament' in the title of this book refers to.

* * *

My entering the *Twittersphere* was rather late, only about two years ago. On entering that labyrinth one discovers many different types of gravitation pull and tendencies: from vital exchanges of information offered in good faith and with probity, fellowship, emotional support and reassuring integrity all the way to narcissistic idiosyncrasy and the anger and invective of those entrenched in a certain world view. Perhaps the political class should be thankful for this channel which when it forms a chamber of rage, stops it becoming a path towards them. *Twitter*, at its worst, can seem as if it is a manifestation of the vision towards the end of Dostoyevsky's *Crime and Punishment*:

> *'Some new sorts of microbes were attacking the bodies of men, but these microbes were endowed with intelligence and will. Men attacked by them became at once mad and furious. But never had men considered themselves so intellectual and so completely in possession of the truth as these sufferers, never had they considered their decisions, their scientific conclusions, their moral convictions so infallible. Whole villages, whole towns and peoples went mad from the infection. All were excited and did not understand one another. Each thought that he alone had the truth and was wretched looking at the others, beat himself on the breast, wept, and wrung his hands. They did not know how to judge and could not agree what to consider evil and what good; they did not know whom to blame, whom to justify.'*

I was one of those initially infected, to a degree, with this microbe as I fulsomely expressed my anger, especially towards those propagating the 'antisemitism crisis' narrative. Just as I handed it out so did invective flow liberally in my direction -I was an *antisemite* myself, a *Kapo* and of course a *self-hating Jew*. These insults were the standard ones applied to Jews who would not accept the narrative and vigorously challenged it. The aforementioned *"AsAJew"* label was applied to me many times. In time, I realised that my anger only fuelled and entrenched the binary opposition which was the very thing I wanted to challenge and loosen, so I gradually calmed down and tried to focus on possible dialogue however unlikely it was to be able to establish it. I also learnt a great deal from others who had been challenging the narrative for some time prior to my arrival. I am grateful to them. Some are mentioned in this study. Eventually I weaned myself off *Twitter* using it as a source of information rather than a vehicle of engagement, dipping in from time to time then moving back out. It seems a great paradox that as the abundance of information available to us on social media became as numerous, although not as discreet, as Saharan grains of sand, the Babel-like result, so similar to Raskolnikov's dream partially quoted above, acted as a sort of Paul Klee-like *'Zwitscher-Maschine'* operating entirely independently from any political change.

At the present time, the forty-year human laboratory experiment of wealth-siphoning neoliberalism seems to be morphing into a form of fascism, summoning identarian politics, the sentimentalisation of 'the family unit' and a hypertrophied *'my house (and a few buy-to-lets) is my castle'* ideology. It as if the neoliberal obsession with the American Dream and an *'I stand on my own two feet owing nothing to anyone'* stance has created, because of the human energy it consumes, a form of resentment that has fed a desire to exercise revenge through manifesting an exaggerated belief in that very system. In other words, those that have laboured years to, ostensibly, *make it* and realise they have been left with a handful of marbles dare not admit they were scammed all along but must pretend those marbles are the riches of Croesus whilst inhaling the heady, mephitic vapours of cheap *Schadenfreude* as compensation to further prop up the deception. This grotesque callousing of society, the main product of driving people into a collective frenzy of forced self-interest, has resulted in a bizarre form of inverse *'survivors syndrome'* combined with a denialism that pushes away any potential realisation that the system that is flogging them is actually not worth the candle, at least for most people. Yet the drive to perpetuate it persists. Whilst in speculative mode, it might be worth considering whether the underlying dissatisfaction, often suppressed, is that the system we are propping up has not delivered the 'goods' we expected or have been made to believe were expected. It has, rather, delivered a hell of a lot of 'bads.'

Despite the arguable futility of publishing anything in a culture glutted with information and seeming rather burnt out and tired of itself, I decided to plough ahead and add my own voice if only to register the melancholy of loss, a loss that probably started to manifest itself many years ago although I was only vaguely conscious of it at the time. One of my first jobs was working on a project to set up the *Manchester Jewish Museum* in the North of England which was, largely, focused on the social and economic history of the Jewish communities in Manchester. While working there, I had the privilege to meet some people who might well have appeared in the photograph at the top of the front cover of this book. By the time I met them, they were, of course, aged but their memories still sharp. They talked of their experiences going over to Spain to fight fascism as if it had been a perfectly natural thing to do at the time. And now they were living in a world rapidly being ushered into neoliberalism, an experiment that was to last forty years. Now, those people I spoke to about their memories from the 1930's all those years ago seem a sharp but distant memory to me.

Governments in the West now seem strangely farcical, as if they have become, as we noted earlier, a sort of pastiche. As if all that is left is to operate like a cheap imitation of something that is a relic of an earlier period. The leverage of antisemitism for political purposes, as I have argued, also had a quality and aura of pastiche about it, the meaning cheapened and abused, while real antisemites such as Johnson and Trump were seen as friends of Jews. One now expects caricature as the norm in a society where hundreds of thousands can die as a result of economic ideology and the tragedy of antisemitism is used as a mechanism to obstruct changes that might alleviate that very present tragedy.

As a concluding section to this concluding section, I'd like to bring up the issue of mental health and its role in the antagonism's expressed around the 'new antisemitism' and the supposed crisis in the Labour Party. As I mentioned in the acknowledgements at the start of this book, I have struggled with mental health issues for most of my life. Mental health is, paradoxically, much easier to talk about now compared to when I was a young man. I say 'paradoxically' because this openness has developed in tandem with a neoliberalism that has arguably exacerbated this very issue. A recent article in *The Independent* stated that waiting lists for support and care had reached 1.2 million with the mental health charity MIND saying that 'we are now seeing the cumulative result of years of underfunding combined with overwhelming demand for mental health.'[12] This is illustrative of the paradox of neoliberalism: create a patina of openness and progressiveness whilst underneath this wafer thin layer maintain a cruel and thuggish financialised system that militates against it.

It was saddening how often the use of mental health slurs came up in clashes between those defending the antisemitism narrative and those questioning it. These slurs were usually directed at those challenging the dominant narrative whose marginality was, in this way made to seem a product of mental health problems. Typical of this and only in a slightly more sophisticated form were Jewish writer, Howard Jacobson's remarks in a *Jewish Chronicle* interview back in 2010. Jacobson had been a torch bearer for the 'new antisemitism' orthodoxy for some years and carried this lambent flame through the post 2015 years, adding his rather garrulous and puggish offerings and his penny-bazaar observations with a predictable regularity. In the *Jewish Chronicle* interview he scrapes the barrel further, or perhaps explores its underside with the following remarks concerning anti-Zionist Jews:

> *'When it comes to Jewish anti-Zionists, their Jew-hatred is barely disguised, not in what they say about Israel but in the contempt they show for the motives and feelings of fellow-Jews who do not think as they do...let's call the thing that drives us by its proper name. Hiding behind Israel is a cowardly way for a Jew to express his anti-Jewishness. That half the time he[sic] is battling his [sic] psychic daddy and not his psychic homeland I don't doubt, though I accept that, in political discourse, we have to pretend that what we are talking about is what we are talking about.'* [13]

Jacobson's characteristic surly tone, the cocky self-assuredness which results in him displaying the very quality of contempt he is ostensibly

12 https://www.independent.co.uk/news/health/nhs-mental-health-waiting-list-b2145432.html

13 Quoted in Kahn-Harris, op. cit.

seeing in others, hoists himself by his own petard. He perorates with crude slurs about the putative mental health of those Jews of whom he is being critical. Simultaneously and implicitly, he arrogates to himself the right to be declared as having a totally clean bill of health psychologically, his motives emanating from a place of immaculate purity and source of 'truth' without the slightest hints of projection. As Jacobson wants to call things by their 'proper name,' let's call this what it is: bullying. Attributing poor mental health to those that disagree with you is a typical authoritarian stance and has a certain history of use by regimes of that ilk.

Perhaps publication of this book may bring out similar responses from some that read it, especially as I have openly acknowledged my own mental health struggles. My acknowledgement of them was not about making any virtue of vulnerabilities as such but in order to contribute to a culture of readiness to be open about these struggles and send some signal of solidarity to those that struggle likewise. The *'AsAJew,' 'fake Jew.'* *'kapo,' 'self-hating Jew,' 'battling his psychic daddy'* vilifications are crude epithets that not only firm up binary simplifications but dehumanise the other and do not redound to the credit of those using them. Those that have unquestioningly propped up the 'antisemitism narrative' often posit themselves as those that dwell in that famed arbour of 'common sense,' a self-defined, apodictic world that axiomatically brooks no dissent. I hope that I may have at least got across to readers why this very stance is, essentially, un-Jewish. I hope I have learned from my own phase of *Twitter*-anger that it is, ultimately, counterproductive and only exacerbates the confrontational stance. There are reasons to be upset and angry but there is also something in the nature of our political and economic system that benefits from us all hollering at one another.

Annex 1

The Anatomy of a Labour Party Apparatchik

Earlier this year (2022), I wrote to the Labour M.P of the constituency in which I live (I hesitate to refer to the M.P as *'my'* Labour M.P) expressing my concern that Jewish M.Ps had not objected to the use of a further accusation of antisemitism against Jeremy Corbyn in a letter by then Home Secretary Nadhim Zahawi, praising Boris Johnson as he was about to depart, in which he stated that Johnson had *'saved'* the country from a *'dangerous antisemite.'* Whether the adjective 'dangerous' referred to Corbyn's 'danger' as a challenger of the vested interests of people like Nadhim Zahawi, or whether it was a mere intensifier of the antisemitism smear remains unclear. What was clear, is that it was a further propagation of the crude leverage of antisemitism, undermining the tragic significance of the word and a knowing exploitation of a vilification that had crescendoed through the previous seven years which was clearly considered an acceptable thing to say or put in print. I thought I would test the M.P., to see whether there was any probity, decency or even a homeopathic residue of freedom of thought left within him. I more or less knew the answer to this without bothering to take the time to go through this procedure but still being surprisingly open to the possibility of the unexpected, I went ahead, sending the following e-mail:

Dear -

As a recent Jewish arrival in your constituency and someone who has been exercised, over the last seven years by the politicised, illiterate leverage of antisemitism that is an insult to those Jews who suffered the real tragedy of it, I am disturbed by the recent use of this smear by one senior Tory, namely Nadhim Zahawi who, as he knifed Johnson in the front, offered him faint praise for keeping out of No 10 'a dangerous antisemite.'

This flagrant lie and abuse of the term has, of course, gone unchallenged by Labour due to their buying into it and now passing it off as 'fact' and beyond debate due to the MSM hammering of it over years. Starmer has fostered the smear as he also plays into the MSM disinformation machine in order to gain acceptance within the establishment.

I have no idea what you believe in your heart of hearts, of course. But surely silence on this matter would be an indictment of collusion with one of the most massaged and pernicious myths of recent political life.

Are you prepared to speak out or collude, or simply shoulder shrug? [1]

It would have been impossible for this M.P to respond with any serious engagement without endangering career and/or losing the whip in a Party whose leader, proven to have misled Party members to an almost pathological degree to get into power, had demanded totall conformity from constituency parties around the antisemitism narrative, closed down any positive debate and obliged his M.P's to be robotically on message. Indeed, during the 2022 Party Conference, any Labour Party front bencher asked about the *Al Jazeera, Labour Files* documentary that further exposed the way antisemitism and other baseless accusations were leveraged and used as a way of destroying members who would not acquiesce to the narrative, responded with a generic "*I'm sorry I have to go now*" before scuttling away.

Within this context it was rather irrational to expect anything that departed from the official line and of course the reply, robotic in content, came a few weeks later reading as if it had been produce by AI and might

---

1   Sent on July 7th 2022

well have been. One can read it almost hearing Starmer's wooden delivery, projected with the characteristic nasal monotony of that disturbingly dead-eyed *golem*:

> *Dear Mr Cohen,*
>
> *Thank you for writing to me about using allegations of antisemitism as political leverage.*
>
> *I agree with you that allegations of antisemitism are extremely serious and should never be used for party political gain. We know where antisemitism can lead and it's vital that every political party challenges it, whenever it rears its ugly head. However, I have also been clear that the allegations of antisemitism under Jeremy Corbyn's leadership were not dealt with properly or fast enough and I was deeply disturbed by the allegations of political influence in disciplinary processes relating to antisemitism.*
>
> *Under Keir Starmer's leadership, I'm pleased the party has improved antisemitism disciplinary processes, committed to training our staff and members on this vile form of racism and has implemented the EHRC Report's recommendations in full. Due to ongoing legal disputes and as Jeremy Corbyn is not a Labour MP, it would be not be appropriate for me to comment on his personal views.*
>
> *I am grateful to you for taking the time to contact me about this matter.[2]*

As will be observed from this 'response,' the thundering condescension and avoidance of any engagement with the question is obvious. And it was entirely predictable. Although responses from M.P.'s about contentious and ideological issues tend to be like this, that is, the parroting of a Party line in its most mechanical form, I had perhaps, as a Jewish constituent,

---

2   Received on August 18th.

harboured the illusion that my concerns about a specifically Jewish issue might have evoked a hint of a more personal response given the M.P was also Jewish. Of course, this was entirely naive of me.

I furnished this M.P with a response that was not entirely free of a rumble of anger and outright sarcasm which seemed the only weapon left and which I knew would terminate the communication:

> *Dear -*
>
> *Many thanks for your reply which, I must say, contained a certain impressive virtuosity which I must acknowledge. I suppose this 'virtuosity' is a prerequisite for survival in the world which you inhabit.*
>
> *First of all, many thanks for avoiding my question entirely and making sure your answer was as neutral and anodyne as possible, leaving the substance unremarked on and left dangling in the air -another demonstration of your supreme talent.*
>
> *Secondly, thank you for ignoring the contents of the Forde Report which made it clear that what you call the 'mishandling of antisemitism complaints' was not simply an issue of leadership interference but the result of (and the report makes it clear there was a Blairite infrastructure largely undermining the LOTO's office) internecine undermining of the leadership's office. Indeed, the report finds no "systemic" attempt by the leadership to interfere and undermine the Party's response to antisemitism. Why are you trying to paint the issue in different colours? (Rhetorical question of course!)*
>
> *Thirdly, your otiose and vapid panegyric to Starmer was a profound insult in the face of the concerns I expressed. I expressed deep concerns about the way Starmer has suspended and effectively vilified Left Wing Jews. You expressed NO concern about where I was coming from*

which I'm sure you actually understood but cast aside as unwonted and irrelevant to the corporate image you need to maintain.. I feel demeaned and insulted because of this.

The response, which showed you up as an utterly craven apparatchik, was of no surprise to me, of course. But the loss of integrity, decency and humanity is deeply saddening.

Yours in gut wrenching disgust

I frequently sign off with the phrase '*yours in gut wrenching disgust*' when dealing with vapid and robotic responses from apparatchiks who are spouting some corporate standpoint or official narrative. I am old enough to remember the Labour Party of the 70's where there was a rich array of views especially around the debate on joining what was then the European Economic Union. But now it was all about keeping the Party hermetically sealed and returned to its place as being only the distance of a sheet of graphene from the one in power. The one party state had been safely reinstalled.

The Corbyn period was an ultimately a failed attempt to increase democracy at the local level. The above interchange now shows how closed down the culture actually is and how any questioning of the shocking disinformation campaign which included the most cheap and ghastly leveraging of antisemitism, has been utterly crushed. The M.P's claim that there was a legal case that prevented him commenting seems otiose. The only legal case current at the time was a libel case brought by the political blogger Richard Millet that was dropped in September 2022. It had no connection with the Labour Party. He could have easily commented in a way that related to my concern without it touching upon that very specific case. No case was still extant that could have prevented the M.P from commenting as far as I am aware. The notion that he also could not comment because Corbyn was technically not a Labour M.P was also a redundant statement: the M.P. had worked under him and ostensibly supported him. This seemed to me to be another coded message conveying that he was obliged to be *shtum* on the issue in order to preserve the stale narrative: that which could ne'er be questioned. It was also clear that he was keeping a narrative going unmodified by the *Forde Report* which, as I point out in my response, challenged the notions he was mechanically repeating. But the media silence on that report was almost total and this M.P was not about to break it.

It now seems very clear that what we call 'the establishment' has, in some way, used Starmer as a medium for rendering the Labour Party compliant with its interests[3] whilst appearing a token opposition. It appears that the major political Parties in the UK are now thoroughly authoritarian and barely need members any more, or even need to show any cognisance of their existence. It seems these Parties are now ciphers for the preservation of a system that was so under threat of change from 2015-2019 that any chance of this repeating itself had to be closed down. The speed and vehemence with which Starmer closed down democracy in the Labour Party, created Shibboleths around NATO, non-attendance on picket lines and of course the maintenance of the antisemitism narrative, was proportionate to the establishment's horror of radical change that was allowed to slide in through a loophole. That eye of the needle had to be very quickly cemented up.

It seems reasonable to assume that the continuous cementing in of the antisemitism narrative is essential to the maintenance of the wider disinformation campaign. Were it to noticeably slip then it could threaten the whole house of cards of mis- and disinformation that has saturated politics in recent years.

---

3   See: https://novaramedia.com/2021/03/02/keir-starmer-is-a-long-time-servant-of-the-british-security-state/ *'much of his work as DPP blurred the boundaries between prosecutor and politician – following the dictates of the Cameron coalition, negotiating with foreign officials on its behalf, and dropping or pursuing cases according to its interests. In so doing, Starmer was integrated into the national security establishment. The nationalist-militarist tone of his Labour leadership may be partially determined by political expediency – but it is also a reflection of this wider history. As such, it is unlikely to yield to pressure from below.'*

Annex 2

The anatomy of distraction, displacement and decoy

Despite my poor health, suffering from M.E and struggling with mental health issues, largely dominated by an intractable O.C.D which turned everyday into a challenging obstacle course as my mind scurried around its own contents trying, in vain, to find a place of psychological safety, I pushed myself to my limits campaigning for a Labour victory in 2019. A sense that the whole project for systemic change was slipping away was getting stronger from the beginning of that year as the Brexit-Remain culture war took hold as an immense decoy, taking the spotlight off issues of economic ideology leaving an infantile tit-for-tatting game that must have delighted the corridors of power and the 'money-shufflers.' The culture war '*furphy*' was to dominate the whole election period.

As the general election approached I accompanied the Labour candidate for my area on some hustings. On one occasion, we visited a working men's club (a term I thought was no longer in use), set up stall in an upstairs room and waited to see who would turn up. There was a large table in the room, the sort of table that might be used for a committee meeting. On our way in we had noticed that there was a group of men in the bar area, now below us, who gave the impression they were out for the day intent on doing some reasonably heavy drinking. There were signs of a certain volubility and vocal volume that signified possible volatility. We sat down awaiting anyone who wanted to talk to us about the up coming election and the issues connected with it. Suddenly, this group, entirely male, entered the room and filled all the seats around the table, pint glasses firmly placed in front of them as if they meant some sort of business. We felt a little intimidated. The atmosphere felt hostile and we were not in a constituency where Labour had been historically strong but now had the additional animus of the pumped up culture war that had, predictably, worked against the Party. I, for one was anticipating a sustained wave of mockery and invective. As an ex-secondary school teacher I felt that my experience gave me some preparation for dealing with conflict, should it arise and took the initiative to engage with them. It turned out to be less hostile than I at first thought. The group members, defining themselves categorically as ordinary 'workers' who 'grafted' for a living as carpenters ('chippies') on building sites, although very assertive in their stance and somewhat self-righteous in their self-presentation as -salt-of-the-earth types weren't being gratuitously rude, at least at first. I had put myself forward as the main interlocutor from our group, partly out of a desire to offer some sort of 'diplomatic bridge' and challenge a stance that I had already assumed from general demeanour and body language was likely to be propping up the populist side of the Brexit/Remain culture war 'decoy' and partly, as I have said, because I felt I could apply techniques I had learnt in years of battling it out in classrooms. The challenge for me, of course was not to sound like I was propping up either side in any way. The following snippets of the dialogue that ensued are paraphrases but remain accurate as to essential content:

Group member: "We're workers! Why can't he [*referring to Corbyn[1]*] just leave [*referring to the Brexit debacle*]

Myself: "He did support 'Leave' but there have been too many pressures from other elements in the Party. I agree about leaving but you need the right policies alongside leaving; leaving on its own without any big policy changes won't do much."

There was a short collective silence at this point before another group member spoke out in a rather cocksure tone:

Group member: "I suppose you are all middle class types with big houses."

Myself: "Well, I live in a Housing Association House because I couldn't afford to buy, especially in this area."

Group Member: "Oh, so you're a scrounger then."

---

1   Corbyn was, essentially a 'Lexiter.' that its, supporting an exit from the E.U from a Left perspective. He later stated he voted Remain whilst being critical of the EU structures and austerity bias.

I smiled a sort of mechanical smile of forbearance at that point. The put down was straight from the propaganda play book that the Government had been using for years and that short interaction contained, in compressed form, almost all the canards and caricature clichés that had formed around the in work, property owner, martyred-by-mortgage, 'standing-on-their-own-two-feet regular 'yeoman" versus anyone vulnerable or needing a helping hand. The man's somewhat cavilling and mocking tone was hurtful to me personally, as I fell, at that stage in my life, very much into the latter group. I had to work hard to remain composed and affable. The next interaction offered more on the theme of the sanctimoniousness of the property owner and guardian of the family-as-fortress. It deepened my sense of how much callousing and lack of any collegial sensibility seemed to be dominant now and the deeply depressing sense of the incipient proto-fascism that this anger towards the vulnerable contained. The group members started to converse amongst themselves and while this happened, a rather quietly spoken man from the group beckoned to me in a surprisingly soft, solicitous way that belied the harshness of the stance he was about to evince, indicating he wanted me to sit near him to discuss a personal issue that was exercising him:

The Man: "Can I have a word with you about something?"

Me: "Yes, go ahead."

The Man: "I've got a house that's worth £300,000, I've had to work hard for it but now I've got something to pass on to my family."

Me: "That's good, you have done well for yourself there."

The Man: "Yes but the bloke next door doesn't work but he gets to live in that house which is like mine...that's not fair is it?"

Me: "But you've got the house, you've got something that's worth £300000 and that chap has got nothing, zero. Nothing to pass to his kids- you've done better than him!"

The Man: "Yeah, I understand what you are saying but he's still living there, isn't he?"

Me: "Yes, he gets some benefit from it but you've got the wealth, he hasn't."

The Man: "But he's still living there."

Me: "But he needs to live somewhere"

The Man: "But why can't the council put him somewhere else, like in a cheaper house in an area that's not so good."

I could sense the animosity that this man felt to his neighbour and felt deeply uncomfortable. The man clearly could not bear this neighbour and his family being in a similar house to him, a fact which seemed to threaten the status of his own achievement. I'd assumed that this man's hated neighbour was probably ill and he considered him to be faking it in some way. This was another sentiment that had been induced by Governments for some years, that most people's illnesses were faked or imaginary and that there was, most likely, no such thing as illness at all. Again, the sort of government manipulated sentiment that could lead, as we observed in the introduction, to vilification and even attacks on ill and vulnerable people. Note the emotion around his perception of himself as protector of *his* family. The use of *the family* as an emotionally loaded sentiment has been a significant element in right wing, populist discourse, recently taken up by Starmer's Labour Party as it tries to appropriate populism for itself. The phrase *hard working families* was often on the lips of manipulative and condescending politicians as they patted the populace on the head for buying into their wealth syphoning model which was largely a Sisyphean task for many trying to keep up with a mortgage on a stagnating wage which now, through inflation, is further reduced in value. The notion of the 'family as fortress' is the sort of lynch pin of a financialised world where not only the individual maximises self interest but it is inscribed on the escutcheon of each household, compounding the *bellum omnium contra omnes*. Blake's words come to mind here:

> *Is this thy soft Family-Love,*
> *Thy cruel patriarchal pride;*
> *Planting thy family alone,*
> *Destroying all the world beside.*[2]

I found it was impossible to try to explain it in systemic terms, the emotional appeal of seeing one's neighbour as the problem and dehumanising the other through scapegoating had too strong a pull. Yet the man's feelings *were* understandable, though not justifiable: he seemed to be consumed by an anger, in this case very justifiable, that he had had to struggle for years, working hard, for his house and the betterment of his

---

2   William Blake: Jerusalem: *The Emanation of Giant Albion.* Chapter 2.

family as he saw it and saw someone, apparently escaping that treadmill, albeit poor, which raised questions, questions that were undermining of his life of work that devoted years to driving a mortgage up the hill. That these men were hale and hearty and had the health to hold down a physically demanding job with a wage, I learnt later, of nearly three times the national average did not seem to lessen the animosity. For me, it was ironically significant that this man's work, on a building site, was at the epicentre of the very industry that gave him his wealth whilst simultaneously wrecking the real economy via the asset bubble it rode on, creating the need for large Housing Benefit payments, often for those in work. If people on Housing Benefit felt threatening to the meaningfulness of work and of his sweated mortgage, then questions needed to be asked about the very industry for which he was working that was embedded in an asset bubble paradigm, was breaking up communities and arguably creating a mental health crisis[3] through the stress it created for so many millions. But emotions are not easily channelled in such a direction. I made no attempt to go into any of these issues.

The economist, Fred Harrison, has written about the deleterious effects of land and housing bubbles on whole cultures and societies, about how it affects the well being of the community at large, siphons wealth to the financial and financialised sectors and in the end undermines the very economic life on which it lives parasitically. It can even lead to societal collapse and war.[4] Unfortunately, it is very difficult to change the dynamic as long as there are enough people who appear to be benefiting from it and who, due to the psychological impact of neoliberalism creating the impetus to model oneself as '*an agent of the maximalisation of self-interest,*' will not be able to see beyond the apparent localised 'benefit' in order to link it with the broader economic pathology. The man who spoke to me about his hatred of his neighbour who seemed to be implicitly undermining the value of his life's work, was, of course, equally unable to do this.

Why have I included this cameo of an encounter during the last General election campaign? And what does it have to do with the issue

---

3   For a good account of the connection between the housing crisis in the UK and mental health on a personal and systemic level see: https://novaramedia.com/2021/07/22/housing-security-transformed-my-mental-health/

4   See: Fred Harrison, *The Traumatised Society.*

of the leverage of antisemitism which this book is really about? Well, as I argued in the introduction, I felt there was a need to present the leveraging of antisemitism within the broader economic context rather than as an isolated and idiosyncratic phenomenon that could be only seen *sui generis.* For me, the use of decoys, displacements and distractions were all of a piece, all designed to undermine any fundamental change. The false narratives, exploitation of emotions, whether it be the 'hard working family' trope or the 'Zionism equals Jews and Judaism' trope all became part and parcel of the 'disinformation paradigm' that was propping up a damaging status quo that desired its self-preservation. And now, as I bring this text to a close, we have other tropes floating over our heads- that of the 'unprovoked war in Ukraine' and 'NATO defending our values.' In the UK, those 'values' led to some 330000 excess deaths connected with our economic ideology. Some values to defend!

In conclusion, my encounter with the group of 'chippies' revealed to me and still reveals to me as I ponder it, a reality that had largely eluded me. I now realise that neoliberalism wasn't just an ideology that was imposed on a society that underneath its mechanisms remained largely attached to the values it had prior to the neoliberal mantle descending upon it. Rather, that neoliberalism's behavioural and attitudinal matrix had created a change in thought and feeling by its adamantine imperatives. It was this latter I had failed to fully comprehend which was why, as I related in the introduction, I was shocked multiple times by what the last ten years have fully revealed. I'm still shocked by it all. The ugliness became more manifest as if the hideousness of Mephistopheles, until now in a relatively benign guise as demanded by Faustus had revealed itself in its full reality.

Discovering you are living in a world that is different from your imaginings is, perhaps, no bad thing. It's better to be awake than asleep or in a semi-somnolent state however discomfiting it might be. The previous five years had certainly woken me up, by stages, to a world that seemed to be full of a lot of anger, indifference and people clinging to 'their patch' for dear life as well as those who were very satisfied with how they had surfed the whole set up. Yet as well, there were people running food banks, places where people could get meals, Gurdwaras and Mosques and Synagogues making food for local communities regardless of religion or ethnic label. It was clear that collegiality was not dead. But this collegiality was often condescendingly patted on the head by those in power, embedded themselves in financialisation, as some nice civic 'add-on,' a contingent, 'value added' element. A Tory M.P. in 2017, himself embedded in financialisation and global money markets, replete with requisite plummy tone, referred to this 'value added' as "rather uplifting and shows what a good, compassionate country we are." The paternalistic tone and infantilising attitude from someone who had benefited from the very wealth siphoning that was behind the need for such support was quite extraordinary, yet perfectly normalised and not considered outré. It was pastiche, of course. More obvious absurdity.

www.ingramcontent.com/pod-product-compliance
Lightning Source LLC
Chambersburg PA
CBHW052030030426

42337CB00027B/4935